This Book Belongs to...

Book 8

Content and Artwork by **Gooseberry Patch Company**

LEISURE ARTS
Vice President and Editor-in-Chief: Sandra Graham Case
Executive Publications Director: Cheryl Nodine Gunnells
Designer Relations Director: Debra Nettles
Senior Publications Director: Susan White Sullivan
Craft Publications Director: Deb Moore
Design Director: Cyndi Hansen
Special Projects Director: Susan Frantz Wiles
Art Operations Director: Jeff Curtis
Retail Marketing Director: Stephen Wilson

EDITORIAL STAFF
TECHNICAL
Senior Technical Writer: Christina Kirkendoll
Technical Writers: Joyce Scott Harris, Laura Siar Holyfield and
   Jennifer S. Hutchings
Technical Associates: Sarah J. Green and Lois J. Long

EDITORIAL
Senior Editorial Writer: Susan McManus Johnson
Contributing Editorial Writer: Suzie Puckett

FOODS
Foods Associate Editor: Laura Siar Holyfield
Contributing Test Kitchen Staff: Rose Glass Klein

OXMOOR HOUSE
Editor-in-Chief: Nancy Fitzpatrick Wyatt
Executive Editor: Susan Carlisle Payne
Foods Editor: Kelly Hooper Troiano
Director of Photography: Jim Bathie
Senior Photo Stylist: Kay E. Clarke
Test Kitchens Director: Elizabeth Tyler Austin
Test Kitchens Assistant Director: Julie Christopher
Test Kitchens Staff: Kristi Carter, Nicole Lee Faber, Kathleen Royal
   Phillips, Elise Weiss and Kelley Self Wilton
Contributing Photographer: Lee Harrelson
Contributing Photo Stylists: Lydia DeGaris Pursell, Mindy Shapiro
   and Katie Stoddard

DESIGN
Design Captain: Becky Werle
Designers: Tonya Bradford Bates, Kim Kern, Kelly Reider, Anne
   Pulliam Stocks and Lori Wenger

ART
Art Publications Director: Rhonda Hodge Shelby
Art Imaging Director: Mark Hawkins
Art Category Manager: Lora Puls
Lead Graphic Artist: Elaine Wheat
Graphic Artists: Lee Ann Bell and Stephanie Hamling
Imaging Technicians: Brian Hall, Stephanie Johnson and Mark Potter
Photo Stylists: Cassie Francioni and Karen Hall
Contributing Photo Stylists: Sondra Daniel, Christy Myers
   and Jan Nobles
Photographer: Lloyd Litsey
Publishing Systems Administrator: Becky Riddle
Publishing Systems Assistants: Clint Hanson, Josh Hyatt
   and John Rose

BUSINESS STAFF
Vice President and Chief Operations Officer: Tom Siebenmorgen
Corporate Planning and Development Director:
   Laticia Mull Dittrich
Vice President, Sales and Marketing: Pam Stebbins
National Accounts Director: Martha Adams
Sales and Services Director: Margaret Reinold
Vice President, Operations: Jim Dittrich
Comptroller, Operations: Rob Thieme
Retail Customer Service Manager: Stan Raynor
Print Production Manager: Fred F. Pruss

Library of Congress Catalog Number 99-71586
Hardcover ISBN 1-57486-527-7
Softcover ISBN 1-57486-528-5

10 9 8 7 6 5 4 3 2 1

Christmas

Book 8

GOODNESS SAKE.

A LEISURE ARTS PUBLICATION

Christmas

Gooseberry Patch

To all our friends and family…
you fill Christmas with love, warmth and magic!

How Did Gooseberry Patch Get Started?

You may know the story of Gooseberry Patch...the tale of two country friends who decided one day over the backyard fence to try their hands at the mail order business. Started in JoAnn's kitchen back in 1984, Vickie & JoAnn's dream of a "Country Store in Your Mailbox" has grown and grown to a 96-page catalog with over 400 products, including cookie cutters, Santas, snowmen, gift baskets, angels and our very own line of cookbooks! What an adventure for two country friends!

Through our catalogs and books, Gooseberry Patch has met country friends from all over the world. While sharing letters and phone calls, we found that our friends love to cook, decorate, garden and craft. We've created Kate, Holly & Mary Elizabeth to represent these devoted friends who live and love the country lifestyle the way we do. They're just like you & me... they're our "Country Friends®!"

Your friends at Gooseberry Patch

Mary Elizabeth ★ Holly ★ Kate ★ Spot

Table of Contents

Memories of the Season

Come Home for Christmas

Simple Pleasures to Share

Kitchen creations to share

Seasoned greetings

Memories of the season

What are your favorite recollections of Christmas? Do you remember wearing your grandmother's apron while helping her make holiday treats? Maybe it's the memory of bundling up and piling into the car to see the neighborhood lights? Or do you find yourself recalling that first Christmas away from home, when you discovered that friends could be almost as dear as family? Keep those memories bright and shining with these clever ideas. Your thoughtfulness will be appreciated by all your loved ones for many years to come!

Many years have gone by since these star-shaped decorations twinkled atop a Christmas tree, but they continue to sparkle surrounded by fresh-cut greenery. For a festive display, make your own holiday collectibles part of an evergreen arrangement.

open a box full of *sweet* memories

Start a new holiday tradition that everyone in the family can enjoy. Have each person write down their favorite memory of the season, then put their notes in a Christmas Memory Box. As each Yuletide arrives, bring out the box and read the old notes before adding new ones. Instructions to make your memory keeper are on page 122.

Cheery Gift Tag Ornaments are more than just another pretty way to label packages. Make one for each member of your family and they'll have a new ornament for next year's Christmas tree. You'll find the instructions on page 122.

Put a new spin on a ribbon memory board by arranging the ribbons into a snowflake design! What a great way to keep track of holiday party invitations, cards and photos.

"It's Christmas in the mansion,
Yule-log fires and silken frocks;
It's Christmas in the cottage,
Mother's filling little socks;
It's Christmas on the highway,
in the thronging, busy mart.
But the dearest truest Christmas,
is the Christmas in the heart."

— Unknown

Christmas~
that magic blanket
that wraps itself
around us....

AUGUSTA RUNDEL

When you look at your life, the greatest happinesses are family happinesses.
~JOYCE BROTHERS

An *Accordion-Fold Album* holds lots of sweet reminiscences in a small space, making it perfect to tuck into a scrapbook or a large stocking. Turn to page 122 to begin this fun project.

My grandmother has a journal that she has had for as long as I can remember. This journal is brought out every year at Christmas and placed next to her chair in the living room. It contains memories from Christmases in our family for the past 20 years. Each year, we take turns reading through the pages, each of us remembering something different as we look through. After looking the book over, we each try to write a little something about this year's happenings so that we can reflect on them again in the coming years. This year, I get to write about my first baby's first Christmas. And someday I know she will be able to look back and read exactly how I was feeling that day. I think that's pretty special.

— Jennifer Smith
Manchester, CT

More than Santa, *your sister knows when you've been* BAD and GOOD. —LINDA SUNSHINE

THE Best PReSeNt

From Santa

EMMA

adorable

puppy love

CHRiSTMAS

Does your family have a favorite dish that is a "must-have" at Christmastime? Frame that famous recipe along with a photo of the much-loved cook who first introduced it to your celebrations. Read all about this delicious idea on page 122.

Sometimes it's the smaller souvenirs that really bring back special memories. Try placing a single ornament, a greeting card or a holiday photograph inside a paperweight.

A small photo in a large frame? Give the photo a clever mat of vintage buttons...lovely!

Candied apples

8 COOKING APPLES (we like ROME APPLES)
1 3/4 C. SUGAR
3/4 C. WATER
9·OZ. PKG. SMALL RED CINNAMON CANDIES

Peel, core and cut apples into eighths. In a Dutch oven, combine sugar, water and candies. Stirring constantly, cook over medium heat about 10 minutes or 'til candies dissolve. Add apples and bring to a boil. Cook about 7 minutes until apples are tender. Cool; cover and store in refrigerator. Serve chilled. Makes 6½ cups.

When I decided to use a bare-branched sweet gum tree covered in "snow," instead of a Christmas tree, I tried for weeks to remember how my talented mother, who passed away many years ago, made the snow out of common household ingredients. No one in our family could remember, either! The day before friends were coming to lunch, I sat down, slightly panicked, to eat my breakfast toast. I picked up a cookbook that happened to be on the kitchen table; it was a book I never used and had placed in a stack to donate to a charity. The book fell open to the very page that told how to mix 2 cups Ivory Snow with 1/2 cup water to make "snow." "Thank you, Mama," I said. "That was close!"

— Wanda Scott Wilson
Hamilton, GA

Every year during the last few days before Christmas, we make a new "Memory List." The list has questions that stay the same, but with four children, our answers differ each year. Some examples of questions are favorite food, favorite song, best friend, teacher, and what do you want to be when you grow up. We also add a new question every year. As we write our new list, we review the old year's answers. We laugh and laugh, and it's a highlight of mine that I wait for each year.

— Tammy Young
St. Peters, MO

NESTLE A BRIGHT GREEN APPLE IN A BOX OR BOWL FULL OF PEPPERMINTS!

12 Tags of Christmas

Celebrate the holidays by making "The 12 Tags of Christmas." The clever designs are simple to craft so children can get in on the fun! Kids will especially enjoy whipping up the oatmeal and glitter Magic Reindeer Mix to give to their classmates. To make these terrific tags, *turn to page 19.*

SleepyTime Tag: Hang one on the door at naptime.

Dear Santa, Here's a bit of help in case you get a tear. From Lori

wishes
Making a list and checking it twice
Merry Xmas

TRADITIONAL CHRISTMAS Memories
f A M I L Y

Holiday Wishes
2006
Just for You

Santa's Favorites are *good* **BOYS and GIRLS** XOXO

DogTag: use dogtreats and a collar to wrap up a tag for your best friend!

Santa's Best Friend

You'll find dozens of uses for these jolly tags! Label presents, trim the Christmas tree, decorate a scrapbook page, serve up a dinner place card…there's even a tag with everything Santa needs to mend his red suit.

THE 12 TAGS OF CHRISTMAS

Standard 2³/₈"x4³/₄" shipping tags were used as the base of each of these tags. Follow our easy suggestions and use your imagination and favorite scrapbook embellishments to make each tag.

MERRY

Pair this tag with the "Christmas" tag below for a unique Christmas greeting. The patterns on page 143 make it easy to recreate this tag. Simply zigzag a fabric "M" to cardstock and color the Santa with colored pencils before adhering them to your tag. Stencil stickers and a few metal embellishments complete your creation.

CHRISTMAS

This tag says it all in one word . . . "Christmas." Make a layered cardstock and fabric "C;" then, finish spelling the word with newsprint stickers and letter tiles. (The "C" pattern is on page 143.) Attach metal stars and string red thread through the hole in the tag.

(continued on page 122)

Color copy nostalgic Christmas postcards...they make such pretty gift tags and jar labels.

19

Come Home for Christmas

Home is where
Christmas dreams come
true, so gather your loved ones
near for a wonderful visit among
these fun and festive decorations.
Friends & family will all agree...from
porch to living room and mantel to
tree, your home at holiday-time
is the best place to be!

*Trimming the snowy tree in style
are a merry mixture of handmade ornaments,
combined with purchased snowflakes and large glass
ball ornaments. Instructions for this winter
wonderland begin on page 23.*

Let It Snow!

The weather outside might be frightful, but frosty decorations inside are delightful! These wintry ideas were inspired by a lucky find at the department store…the little snowman atop the mantel on page 21.

To make Decorative Packages (top) for your mantel, embellish a variety of boxes with scrapbook papers and ribbon. Your holiday fireplace isn't complete until you add Fleece & Chenille Stockings (bottom) in wintry blue and white.
See page 123 to make them cozy with chenille, felt and pom-poms.

DECORATIVE PACKAGES

Use spray adhesive in a well-ventilated area.

Trimming and folding the paper at the corners as necessary, use spray adhesive to cover the boxes and lids with kraft or scrapbook paper. For a snowy lid, spray the lid with adhesive and sprinkle it with mica flakes. Allow the adhesive to dry; then, shake off the excess flakes. Tape or tie ribbon and trim around the packages.

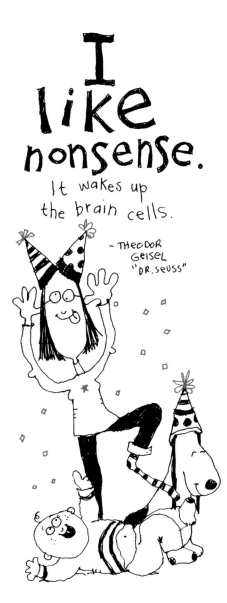

I like nonsense. It wakes up the brain cells.

– THEODOR GEISEL "DR. SEUSS"

CHENILLE STEM ORNAMENTS

CANDY CANES
Twist red and white chenille stems together and bend the ends into a candy cane shape. We found red and white chenille stems that were already twisted together and twisted them together for extra-thick candy canes.

SNOWFLAKES
For each snowflake, twist 3 pieces cut from white bumpy chenille stems together at the center; then, do the same thing with 3 pieces cut from silver chenille stems. Hot glue the pieces together at the center. Hot glue red beads to the centers of the snowflakes.

CLOWN HAT ORNAMENTS
• tracing paper
• assorted scrapbook papers
• double-sided tape
• craft glue
• 1/16"w white satin ribbon
• red and white pom-poms
• assorted embellishments (We used tissue paper, pom-pom trims, rickrack, snowflake and circle punches, cardstock and mica flakes.)

1. For each ornament, use the pattern on page 148 and make a cone hat from scrapbook paper.

2. For the hanger, glue the ends of a 9" ribbon length inside the top of the hat. Glue a pom-pom to the top of the hat.

3. Decorate the hat. (We added pleated tissue paper ruffles, trims, rickrack, cardstock circles and mica-flaked snowflake punch-outs.)

It's not what you look at that matters, it's what you see.

— Henry David Thoreau

This frosty friend is so adorable, he'll warm your heart! Turn to page 124 to make your own too-cute Snowman Chairback Cover. For a whimsical way to bring wintertime fun indoors, fill a large bowl with simple-to-form Yarn Snowballs. Add homemade charm to your gifts by turning to page 125 to make a Noel Gift Tag and a Monogram Gift Tag.

YARN SNOWBALLS

For each snowball, apply a spot of glue on a foam ball. Wrap yarn around the ball and tuck and glue the yarn end under. Arrange the snowballs in a large bowl.

SNOWFLAKE TREE SKIRT

- 1¼ yds of 60"w dark teal fleece
- string
- fabric marking pen
- thumbtack
- tracing paper
- light blue and white felt
- fabric glue
- 3½ yds red pom-pom trim

1. For the skirt, cut a 42" fleece square. Follow *Making a Fabric Circle* on page 142 and use a 19½" string measurement for the outer cutting line. Remove the tack and use a 1" string measurement for the inner cutting line.

2. Cut through all fleece layers along the drawn lines. Unfold the skirt and cut an opening from the outer edge to the center opening.

3. Using the pattern on page 153, cut snowflakes from felt and glue them to the tree skirt. (We used a photocopier to enlarge and reduce the pattern for different-sized snowflakes.)

4. Glue the fringe to the wrong side of the skirt along the outer edge.

Share your wish for peace on earth or joy to the world with handmade greeting cards. But why stop there? Stamped Gift Wrap and the Gift Box with Snowflake Embellishment are two fun ways to make your present just as unique as your cards! Instructions for these happy ideas begin on page 125.

CELEBRATE PACKAGE BANNER

Make a package sparkle with a glittery "CELEBRATE" banner. Die-cut white cardstock letters; then, working in a well-ventilated area, spray adhesive on the letters and sprinkle them with glitter. Once the adhesive has dried, shake off the excess glitter and glue the letters along a length of narrow ribbon. Tie the banner around a package for an extra special gift.

I wish for 5 kittens!

Featuring Santa's red suit, this Ho Ho Ho Card is as jolly as the old elf himself. Send a Wish Card to let someone know that they're never too old to have Christmas wishes. What's a 6-letter word for this Crossword Puzzle Gift Bag...clever! It's the ideal way to present a gift to your favorite crossword enthusiast. Instructions begin on page 126.

ACROSS

5. E. 4 a 3 letter word for happiness
6. Christmas bread
7. Saint Nick
9. door decoration
10. rejoice, party, enjoy, make merry
11. when you ___ upon a star
13. christmas flower
14. famous Snowman
16. Rhymes with Jolly
18. new born King
19. Kiss under this
20. 4 letter word for christmas

DOWN

1. De...
2. le...
3. ___ lo...
7. Hung a chimney w...
8. Custom o... ritual
12. the red-nosed reindeer
15. holiday beverage
17. 4 letter word for christmas

christmas
sweet
dreams
...come true.

27

Naturally Inviting

Transform your entryway into a scene of seasonal delights! Whether you prefer wintry accents or a display of fruit and greenery, one of our four inviting entryways is sure to inspire you to create a welcoming entry full of Yuletide fun! Instructions for this natural setting are on page 127.

Light the way to Christmas cheer with the warm glow of a Candle Centerpiece and snowy Luminaries! With a few simple embellishments, purchased pillows are transformed into Tufted Pillows and a Button Wreath Pillow. The frosty setting provides a welcome spot to reflect on the true reason for the season.

FROSTY
CANDLE CENTERPIECE
Never leave burning candles unattended.

A winter wonderland of button-studded pillar candles, frosty greenery and shiny ornaments make up this shimmering centerpiece. The tray is a large picture frame backed with a thin piece of wood and dry brushed with thinned white acrylic paint. Insert glittered button picks into aqua candles of different sizes and shapes. Arrange button-studded candles and small votive cups holding red candles on the tray. Fill in around the candles with green, pearl and red ornaments. Tuck frosted greenery picks around the bottom of the centerpiece. Sprinkle mica snow over the tray and your centerpiece is complete!

RAILING SWAG
Use floral wire to join frosted greenery picks to form a swag. Loosely wrap the swag with red beaded garland and aqua ribbon. Insert glittered button picks along the swag; then, add aqua, pearl and red ornaments.

(continued on page 128)

For a reminder that Santa's on his way, wire a length of sleigh bells to a fresh greenery wreath…a jolly jingle every time the door opens!

29

APPLES & SPICE

REVERSIBLE THROW

Even a beginner can sew this simple reversible throw. You will need a total of 3½ yards of fleece in various colors. (We used ⅞ yard each of four colors.) Cut 120 total 6" fleece squares. Using a ½" seam allowance, sew the squares into 10 rows of 12 squares each. Sew the rows together, with seams facing the same side of the throw. Fringe the seams and the outer edges of the throw by clipping every ¼".

PATCH PILLOW

To make the matching pillow, you will need ½ yard of fleece in various colors. Cut 18 total 6" fleece squares. Using a ½" seam allowance, sew the squares into 6 rows of 3 squares each. Sew 3 rows together for the pillow front and 3 together for the pillow back. Matching wrong sides, sew the front and back together, leaving one edge open. Insert a 14" square pillow form into the opening and sew it closed. Fringe the edges of the pillow by clipping every ¼".

Spiced Apple Cider

3 QTS. APPLE CIDER
12 WHOLE CLOVES
10 WHOLE ALLSPICE
1 T. CANDIED GINGER
10 CINNAMON STICKS
¾ C. BROWN SUGAR, PACKED

★

COMBINE ALL INGREDIENTS EXCEPT SUGAR AND BOIL. LOWER HEAT, ADD SUGAR AND SIMMER 15 TO 20 MINUTES. STRAIN AND POUR INTO INSULATED CONTAINER TO SERVE STEAMING HOT.

*For a fresh approach to an entryway, place trees in tubs on either side of the door
and fill in the top of each tub with artificial apples.*

TREE CENTERPIECE

- 6" dia. metal bucket
- spray primer
- paintbrushes
- cream and burnt umber acrylic paints
- matte clear acrylic sealer
- kitty litter
- hot glue gun
- boxwood picks
- 17"-tall Christmas tree
- holly picks
- small artificial apples

Allow primer, paint and sealer to dry after each application.

Working in a well-ventilated area, prime the bucket. Dry brush (page 141) the bucket with acrylic paints, apply sealer and fill with kitty litter. Hot glue boxwood picks into the tree until it looks full. Add a few holly picks and apples and place the tree in the bucket.

BOXWOOD MONOGRAM

Tired of wreaths that all look the same? This wreath is sure to be the envy of everyone who sees it! Start by using a computer to print a letter and use a photocopier to enlarge it to the desired size. Draw around the letter onto a 2" thick green floral foam sheet and use a serrated knife to cut it out. For stability, wrap the foam with hardware cloth and secure with floral wire. Insert boxwood picks into the foam, covering the sides and front of the letter. Add some holly picks and an artificial apple to one corner. Make a floral wire hanger on the back of the wreath.

SMALL WREATH

Form a wreath with grapevine wire. Hot glue boxwood picks into the wreath. Decorate the wreath with holly picks and an artificial apple.

BUNDLE UP TIGHT! FLURRIES TONIGHT

SNOWBALLS 5¢

WELCOME

TRADITIONAL

SWAG WITH ORNAMENTS

This traditional decorating theme, featuring greenery and red ribbons, is sure to bring out the holiday spirit in everyone! Begin by cutting a length of garland long enough to swag across the doorway and drape down each side. Wire in pieces of holly. Wrap ribbon around the top of the garland and allow the ends to drape down each side. Tie 2 ribbon bows and wire one to each side of the swag. Wire over-sized ornaments to each side and small ornaments to the center.

DOOR SPRAY

Continue the traditional decorating theme with a matching door spray. Insert artificial greenery picks into the sides and top of a foam brick. Wire in pieces of holly. Wire a bow to the spray. Wire an over-sized ornament below the bow and small ornaments to the spray.

SNOWBALLS FOR SALE

Add a touch of whimsy to your doorstep with a tub of snowballs. To make the snowballs, wrap various sizes of foam balls with batting. Add filler, such as crumpled newspapers, to the bottom of a galvanized tub; then, cover with a layer of batting. Arrange the snowballs on top of the batting.

For the sign, cut a piece of foam core. Write "SNOWBALLS 5¢" on the sign using a black permanent marker. Glue a strip of batting across the top of the sign. Wrap a yardstick with red & white striped fabric and glue the sign to one end. Insert the sign into the tub of snowballs.

Working in a well-ventilated area, spray adhesive on the snowballs, sign and batting in the tub and sprinkle with mica flakes. Spray the snowballs and batting with adhesive again to seal the mica flakes to the surfaces.

DOORMAT

- 18"x30" sisal doormat
- white spray paint
- black permanent marker
- tracing paper
- paintbrush
- red, white and black acrylic paints

Use spray paint in a well-ventilated area. Allow paint to dry after each application.

Coat the mat with white spray paint. Draw a 5"x22" rectangle in the center of the mat with the marker. Using the large diamond pattern on page 155, draw rows of harlequin diamonds across the mat with the marker. Paint alternating diamonds red and the remaining diamonds and rectangle white. Use black paint to spell "WELCOME" in the rectangle. After the paint dries thoroughly, outline everything with the marker.

(continued on page 128)

pray for kindness for all creatures great & small.

HE'S CHECKING HIS LIST!

*Santa Claus is coming to town,
so you'd better be good for goodness sake!
In his gift sack, he has a Christmas tree that's
trimmed with spirited red & white ornaments.
Cheery knit stockings hang from the banister,
and a handrail garland adds a merry touch.
This whimsical scene is sure to fill
your foyer with Yuletide cheer.*

*Santa is checking his list and getting ready to make the season
bright for all good little boys and girls. The jolly gift-giver and his
basket of presents let visitors know that you believe in holiday
magic. Instructions for these festive ideas begin on page 36.*

GOODNESS SAKE.

Nate
Sarah
Mark
Kim
Chris
Bec
John
Tonya
Robert
Kelly
Tom
Cyndi

SANTA'S BAG
(shown on page 35)
For a clever change from the traditional tree skirt, you can make this bag in the blink of an eye! Match the short ends of a 3¹/₈-yard piece of 60"-wide red felt. Sew the sides together, leaving the top open and using a ¹/₂" seam allowance. Press the ends of a 119" length of 1¹/₄"-wide twill tape ¹/₂" to the wrong side and topstitch. For the casing, begin at a side seam and pin the twill tape to the wrong side of the bag, 8" from the top edge. Topstitch the tape to the bag along the long edges. Turn the bag right side out. Open the side seam between the tape ends. Thread a 4¹/₂-yard length of ¹/₂"-diameter cord through the casing. Knot the cord ends and you're ready to bag that tree!

GOODY BASKET
- rectangular basket (ours measures 12"x18"x9")
- red felt
- 1"-tall white self-adhesive felt letters
- fabric glue
- white eyelash trim

Use a ¹/₄" seam allowance for all sewing unless otherwise indicated.

What fun it will be to fill this basket with goodies! For the liner, measure the inside bottom of the basket and add ¹/₂" to each measurement. Cut a felt rectangle the determined size. For each side panel, measure the width of the side and add ¹/₂". Measure the height of the side and add 4¹/₂" for the flap. Cut a piece of felt the determined size. Sew each side panel to the bottom felt piece and sew the sides together. Turn the top edge ¹/₂" to the wrong side

and topstitch. Place the liner in the basket and fold the flap over the rim. Adhere the felt-letter message to the flap. Glue the trim along the inside bottom edge of the flap.

HANDRAIL GARLAND
(shown on page 35)
To spruce up your staircase, weave white eyelash trim and olive green and red ribbons through a greenery garland that you've tied to the handrail. Add frosted holly and greenery picks and you're done!

"Here comes Santa Claus!
Here comes Santa Claus!
Right down Santa Claus Lane!
He's got a bag that is filled with toys for the boys and girls again."
— Gene Autry and Oakley Haldeman

STRIPED KNIT STOCKING

Refer to Knit, page 141, before beginning the project.

FINISHED SIZE: 7¹/₂"x31" (19x78.5 cm)

MATERIALS
Bulky Weight
Novelty Eyelash Yarn
  [1³/₄ ounces, 47 yards
  (50 grams, 43 meters)
  per skein]:
  White - 3 skeins
Bulky Weight Brushed Acrylic Yarn
  [3¹/₂ ounces, 142 yards
  (100 grams, 129 meters)
  per skein]:
  White - 1 skein
Bulky Weight Yarn
  [5 ounces, 255 yards
  (140 grams, 232 meters)
  per skein]:
  Red - 1 skein
Straight knitting needles, size 13
  (9 mm) **or** size needed for gauge
Stitch holders - 3
Yarn needle

GAUGE: Holding one strand of **each** White together, in Stockinette Stitch, 9 sts and 13 rows = 4" (10 cm)

CUFF
Holding two strands of Red together, cast on 36 sts.

Work in K1, P1 ribbing for 7" (18 cm).

LEG
Note: Carry unused yarn **loosely** along edge.

Row 1 (Right side): Holding one strand of **each** White together, knit across.

Row 2: Purl across.

Row 3: Knit across.

Row 4: Purl across.

Row 5: Holding two strands of Red together, knit across.

Row 6: Purl across.

Row 7: Holding one strand of **each** White together, knit across.

Row 8: Purl across.

Row 9: Knit across.

Row 10: Purl across.

Rows 11-64: Repeat Rows 5-10, 9 times.

Cut yarns.

(continued on page 130)

For a fun change, knit these cheery Striped and Dotted stockings and hang them from the staircase instead of the mantel. Instructions for the Dotted Knit Stocking are on page 131.

Wrap bulky weight yarn around foam balls to create Striped and Dotted Ball Ornaments, and remake an old red sweater into Already-Knit Ball Ornaments and Santa's Hat Ornaments. Then wrap up your tree trimming with Package Ornaments.

IT'S HARD TO BE GOOD.

STRIPED AND DOTTED BALL ORNAMENTS

Your kitty may want to join in when you make these fast & fuzzy ornaments! Dab a spot of glue on each foam ball and wrap with white or red bulky weight yarn. Tuck the end and use fabric glue to add yarn stripes or swirled dots. For a hanger, knot a yarn loop around a large-headed pin. Dab glue on the sharp end and insert the pin in the ornament.

SANTA'S HAT ORNAMENTS

For each of these playful ornaments, cut an 8¹/₂"x12" rectangle from a red knit item. Matching the right sides, sew the long edges together. Zigzag around both openings and turn right side out. For the cuff and

pom-pom, follow Santa's Hat Tree Topper, using purchased trim or a 4-stitch-wide by 13¹/₂" long knit band and a 2" diameter foam ball.

ALREADY-KNIT BALL ORNAMENTS

For each ornament, cut a piece with one finished edge from a red sweater to fit around a foam ball. Wrap the piece around the ball with the finished edge at the bottom, and glue the sides together with fabric glue. Use embroidery floss to sew *Running Stitches* (page 140) around each end. Pull the stitches tight and knot. Glue white eyelash trim around the top of the ornament. For a hanger, knot a yarn loop around a large-headed pin. Dab glue on the sharp end and insert the pin in the ornament.

PACKAGE ORNAMENTS

- 3¹/₂"x3¹/₂" and 4¹/₂"x4¹/₂" papier-mâché boxes with lids
- craft glue stick
- white and red wool felt
- green hand-dyed wool
- scallop-edged craft scissors
- craft glue
- ¹/₁₆" dia. hole punch
- ¹/₈"w green variegated ribbon
- red chenille yarn

For each ornament, use a glue stick to adhere the box bottom to the center of a felt piece. Following Fig. 1, cut out the corners and adhere the side flaps to the box sides. Trim any excess felt. Repeat with felt or wool to cover the lid and scallop the edges if desired.

Fig. 1

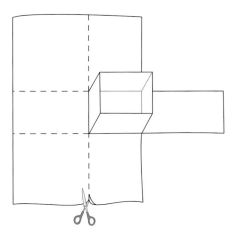

Glue wool or felt circles to the ornament with craft glue, or punch holes in ¹/₂"-wide scallop-edged felt strips and glue the strips and green ribbon lengths to the sides of the box. Tie chenille yarn around each box.

This oh-so-sweet St. Nick (page 129) is sure to bring smiles to every child at heart! Make Santa's list more fun and personal by using names of friends and family members.

SANTA'S HAT TREE TOPPER

(shown on page 35)
- large red sweater
- white bulky weight novelty eyelash yarn
- white bulky weight brushed acrylic yarn
- size 17 (12.75 mm) knitting needles
- white embroidery floss
- 3" dia. foam ball
- fabric glue

Refer to Knit, page 141, before beginning the project, or use purchased trim for the cuff.

Cut the sleeve from the sweater at the shoulder. Zigzag around the raw edge. For the hat cuff, holding the 2 yarns together, knit a 7-stitch-wide by 24" long band. Use white floss to *Whipstitch* (page 140) the cuff to the zigzagged opening.

For the pom-pom, dab glue on the foam ball and wrap it with eyelash yarn. Tuck the end and leave a tail. Use floss to sew *Running Stitches* around the sleeve hem. Pull the stitches tight and knot. Using the tail, tack the pom-pom to the sleeve hem.

MERRY MANTELS

*A crackling fire on the hearth draws everyone near at Christmastime.
To make your mantel oh-so merry, decorate it with one of these
four festive themes. Turn to page 132 to broadcast the glad
tidings with this Newsprint Noel Mantelscape.*

Complete with a
miniature gate bearing
a word of good cheer,
this Christmas Garden
Mantelscape is
naturally inviting.
The peaceful scene
includes tin doves,
a pair of obelisks
and papier-mâché apples.
Instead of stockings,
why not hang these
embellished envelopes
with gift cards tucked
inside? The envelopes
can also hold Christmas
cards received from
friends & family.
Instructions are
on page 133.

Does a rustic holiday retreat sound appealing? There's no need to pack your bags…this Lodge-Inspired Mantelscape is just the ticket! The woodsy scene includes miniature trees, candles wrapped with twigs, old-fashioned sock stockings and an easy-to-make log cabin picture. To create your own lodge look, turn to page 133.

To create your own lodge look, turn to page 133.

...And I told Santa you are the bestest dog I know.

What's more cozy than gathering 'round the fireplace for hot cocoa and a chat? Stencil pine trees and stars on a large, galvanized tub. Fill the tub with wood and set by the fire to save trips out into the blustery evening.

concentrate on finding
your goal, then concentrate
on reaching it. ~MICHAEL
FRIEDSMAN

If your holiday mantel arrangement
isn't as full-looking as you would like,
tie some dinner napkins together, corner
to corner, to create a mantel scarf.

May all your Christmas wishes come true! Shimmering stars make a heavenly backdrop for this Dreamy Mantelscape. Turn to page 134 to add sparkle with embellished candles, glittery letters and tussie-mussie "stockings."

Friends and Fun Ornament PARTY

What better way to kick off the holiday season than by hosting an ornament party? Invite your pals over for lunch and have each one bring as many handcrafted ornaments as there are guests. After lunch, have an ornament exchange. In this section, you'll find lots of great ideas to help you prepare for your party, including a recipe that's sure to make the day a sweet success…homemade chocolate-covered cherries!

You have been INVITED
to have LUNCH
(and some *chocolate covered cherries*- YUM!!)
with your FRIeNdS

Where: LORI'S HOUSE
When: Saturday, December 9, 2006
Time: Noon

We will be **swapping** *handmade* ornaments.
Everyone needs to bring **6** of her ornament.

It's a place to raise your family
And a place to laugh with friends.
It's a place to put your feet up
And rest at the work day's end.

With space to store your treasures
And space to make your own
It's a place to play,
It's a place to love,
It's the place that you call

Home.
-Andrea L. Mack-

ORNAMENT PARTY INVITATIONS

- cream and red cardstock
- stylus
- craft glue
- assorted scrapbook papers
- $1/8$"w red ribbon with white stitching
- decorative-edged craft scissors
- alphabet rub-ons
- metal "O" and "P" charms
- $1/8$" dia. silver brads
- $1/2$"w silver foil tape
- $1/4$" dia. hole punch
- fabric scraps from Hostess Apron (page 46)
- ornament charms
- adhesive foam dots
- $5^1/4$"x$7^1/4$" cream envelopes

For each card, cut a 5"x12" cream cardstock piece . Use the stylus to score across the card 5" from one short edge; fold along the scored line. Use a computer to print party information on another cream cardstock piece. Trim the cardstock to 5"x7" and aligning the top edge with the fold, glue it to the inside card back. Glue a $2^1/2$"x5" paper piece along the bottom edge of the inside back and glue ribbon along the top edge of the paper. Stack and glue paper and cardstock squares on the card front and embellish with cardstock strips, rub-ons, charms, brads and foil tape. Punch two holes, $1/2$" apart, in the center of the paper on the inside card back. Knot a 1"x$6^1/2$" fabric strip through the holes and use a brad to attach the ornament charm to the card through the knot. Secure the charm with a foam dot. Using craft scissors on one long edge, cut a 1"w red cardstock strip and glue it along the opening of each envelope.

Razzle, dazzle, and recycle…paint burned-out light bulbs with glass paint and add swirls or polka dots with a paint pen. Twist florist's wire around the bases, leaving an end to shape into a loop for hanging.

Gather bowls and clear glass vases to pile full of ball-shaped ornaments for a pretty display.

HOSTESS APRON

- 1 yard floral print cotton fabric
- 3 yards of 1¼"w twill tape
- ⅜ yard coordinating fabric for pocket
- paper-backed fusible web
- green, red and white fabric scraps
- green, red and white thread
- ½" dia. black pom-pom

Yardages are based on fabric with a 40" usable width.

Cut a 30"x36" piece from floral fabric. For the top of the apron, follow Fig. 1 to mark a 12" section at the center of one short edge and mark each long edge 14" from the corner. Draw a line connecting the marks on each corner. Cut along the drawn lines.

Fig. 1

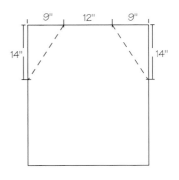

For the hem, press the top edge ³/₈", then ¹/₂" to the wrong side and topstitch. Repeat to hem the straight side edges and the bottom edge. Press the angled side edges ¹/₄", then 1" to the wrong side and topstitch along the pressed edge to make a casing. Press each end of the twill tape ¹/₂" to the wrong side. Fold the twill tape in half, matching the long edges, and topstitch the edges together. Starting at the top, thread the twill tape ends through the casings. Cut a 9"x12¹/₂" piece from the pocket fabric. Press the short edges and one long edge ¹/₂" to the wrong side. For the top of the pocket, press the remaining long edge ³/₈", then ¹/₂" to the wrong side; topstitch. Trace the patterns on page 151 onto the paper side of the fusible web and cut them out. Fuse the patterns to the wrong side of the appropriate fabric scraps. Remove the paper backing; then, arrange and fuse the appliqués on the pocket. Machine satin stitch the appliqués to the pocket. Sew the pom-pom to the flower center. Sew the side and bottom edges of the pocket to the center of the apron front.

Send your friends home with

CHOCOLATE ★ COVERED CHERRIES

16-OZ. PKG. POWDERED SUGAR
¹/₂ C. BUTTER, SOFTENED
1 T. EVAPORATED MILK
2 t. VANILLA EXTRACT
2 10-OZ. JARS MARASCHINO CHERRIES, WITH OR WITHOUT STEMS, DRAINED
12 OZ. CHOCOLATE-FLAVORED CANDY COATING
6-OZ. PKG. SEMI-SWEET CHOCOLATE CHIPS

BLEND TOGETHER SUGAR, BUTTER, EVAPORATED MILK & VANILLA. WRAP EACH CHERRY IN ABOUT 1 TEASPOON SUGAR MIXTURE. ARRANGE ON WAX PAPER IN A BAKING PAN AND CHILL OVERNIGHT. MELT TOGETHER CANDY COATING & CHOCOLATE CHIPS IN A DOUBLE BOILER; STIR UNTIL MELTED AND BLENDED. USE A CANDY DIPPER TO DIP CHERRIES IN CHOCOLATE, TAPPING OFF EXCESS. PLACE ON WAX PAPER TO COOL. MAKES ABOUT 4¹/₂ DOZEN.

End your party on a sweet note with a Christmas classic…chocolate-covered cherries! Send each guest home with a few of the yummy morsels along with a Chocolate-Covered Cherries Recipe Tag. Follow the simple instructions on page 135 to make each tag.

Cover a photo box with cheery fabric; then, monogram and embellish the lid to create a Personalized Ornament Box! Turn to page 135 to get started.

FLOCKED ORNAMENT

- $3/4$" dia. foam brush
- red and green glass paints
- glass ball ornament
- black paint pen
- paintbrush
- SoftFlock® adhesive
- red and green SoftFlock® fibers
- red cardstock
- black fine-point permanent pen
- $1/8$" dia. hole punch
- 12" length of $1/8$"w black ribbon with white stitching

Allow the paint to dry after each application.

Use the foam brush to paint red dots on the ornament for cherries. Use the paint pen to draw stems. Freehand paint green leaves at the top of the stems. Follow the manufacturer's instructions to flock the cherries and leaves. Cut a 1"x1$1/2$" cardstock tag. Write a message on the tag and punch a hole at the top. Remove the wire hanger and cap from the ornament, thread the tag onto the hanger and replace. Knot the ribbon through the hanger.

SANTA ORNAMENT

- craft glue
- peach felt
- 5" dia. foam ball
- white and red fleece
- hot glue gun
- 1/2" dia. pink shank button
- 1/4" dia. black gem stones
- pink chalk
- white faux fur
- 1" dia. silver jingle bell
- 12 1/2" length of 1/4"w red grosgrain ribbon

Glue a 2 1/4"x4" felt piece to the ball for the face. Cut a 2 1/2"x15" white fleece strip for the long layer of the beard. Make 2" long clips, 1/2" apart, for fringe. Hot glue the strip around the ball. Fill in at the bottom with shorter, narrower strips, until the beard is full. For the mustache, fold a 4"x5" white fleece strip in half, matching the long edges. Make 1 1/4" long clips, 3/8" apart, along the long raw edges. Hot glue the strip to the ball, overlapping the face and shaping into a mustache. Hot glue the button and stones to the face for the nose and eyes and add cheeks with chalk. Enlarge the pattern on page 156 to 125%. Using the enlarged pattern, cut a hat from red fleece. Matching the wrong sides, sew the side edges together with a 1/2" seam allowance and turn right side out. Sew a 1 1/2"w fur strip along the bottom edge and the bell to the tip of the hat. Hot glue the hat on Santa's head, covering any exposed edges of the face. Fold the ribbon length in half and glue it to the back of the hat to hang.

The Snowman Tag Ornament and Santa Card Ornament will give your tree whimsical charm. Grab your scrapbooking supplies and turn to pages 135-136 to make the jolly trims.

Simple pleasures to Share

Handmade gifts are
so special…any present that includes
your gift of time and talent is one that's sure
to be cherished. Kate, Holly and Mary Elizabeth
have come up with some great gifts that you'll really
have fun making. A host of accessories will delight the
special women on your list, while a reindeer bath set
and snowman pillow/pajama bag are ideal for little
ones. And what man wouldn't appreciate a special
tray to hold all his valuable pocket items?

*Pretty personalized cards and stationery sets will provide far-away
friends and family a means of keeping in touch throughout the year.*
Instructions for these noteworthy projects and more begin on page 53.

Favorite Things

Send each of your friends a gift that's twice as nice because you made it with them in mind!

A Friendship ATC Gift Card not only shares holiday wishes, but also offers the recipient a collectible Artist Trading Card. To learn more about ATCs, see page 70.

Monograms always lend a personal touch, and these selections are beautiful examples of what you can create for everyone you know. Instructions for the Personalized Tags with Gift Box (above), Boxed Personalized Card Set (opposite, top), and Boxed Green & Brown Stationery Set (opposite, bottom) start on page 136.

FRIENDSHIP ATC GIFT CARD

- 2¹/₂"x3¹/₂" playing card
- craft glue
- ATC background paper or scrapbook paper
- friendship ephemera
- glue dots
- black fine-point permanent pen
- jewelry tag
- brown thread
- ¹/₈" dia. silver brads
- alphabet bottle caps and stamps
- square alphabet brads
- deckle-edged craft scissors
- brown and red cardstock
- variegated brown ink pad
- 6¹/₈" length of ³/₁₆"w ribbon
- 4"x5¹/₂" cream card with square-flap envelope
- black self-adhesive photo corners

See page 70 for more information about ATCs.

For the ATC, cover the playing card with background paper. Cut out and glue pieces of ephemera to the playing card, using glue dots to elevate areas as desired (we used one behind the girl's head). Write a message on the tag. Run thread through the hole in the tag and knot the ends together. Attach the tag and round brads to the ATC. Add bottle-cap and brad initials.

For the card, use the craft scissors to cut a 3⁵/₈"x5¹/₈" brown cardstock piece; ink the edges. Wrapping the ends to the back, glue the ribbon along one long edge of the cardstock. Glue the cardstock to the center of the cream card front. Place photo corners over 2 opposite corners of the ATC and attach it to the cardstock ³/₈" from the bottom. Stamp a message above the ATC.

Glue a ³/₈"w strip of red cardstock, trimmed with the craft scissors, along the bottom edge of the envelope flap.

CARD WITH EARRINGS

- holly and 2½" square border stamps
- green ink pad
- 3½"x4⅞" cream card with square-flap envelope
- craft knife and cutting mat
- colored pencils
- sandpaper
- craft glue
- gold handmade paper
- ⅛" dia. hole punch
- 3½" length of ¼"w cream silk ribbon
- assorted cream beads
- silver beads
- 2½" Bali-style head pins
- crimp beads
- crimp and round-nose pliers
- wire cutters
- 16½" length of ⅛"w green variegated ribbon

Stamp a border in the center of the card front, ⅞" from the top edge. Use the craft knife to cut a 2" square opening in the center of the border. Randomly stamp holly on the outside of the card and color with colored pencils. Lightly sand the outside of the card. Ink the right edge of the card front and the bottom edge of the envelope flap. Glue a 3⅜"x4⅞" handmade paper piece to the inside card back. Punch 2 holes, ½" apart and 1½" from the top edge, in the center of the inside card back. Thread the cream ribbon ends through the holes from front to back. Cross the ends and thread them through the holes again from back to front; trim.

For each earring, thread cream beads and a silver bead onto a head pin as desired. Crimp a crimp bead onto the head pin above the other beads. Use the round-nose pliers to shape the head pin into an earwire. Cut off any excess wire. Attach the earrings through the holes in the inside card back. Wrap the variegated ribbon around the card front at the fold and tie the ends into a bow.

For a timely gift, make this stylish lapel pin that features a watch face. Turn to page 138 to fashion the Brooch with Gift Box.

WOVEN SCARF

Refer to Crochet on page 142 before beginning the project.

Finished Size: 4¹/₂"w x 65"l
(11.5 cm x 165 cm)

 ◼◼◻◻ **EASY**

Materials
Bulky Weight Yarn
   [6 ounces, 185 yards (170
   grams, 169 meters) per ball]:
   Variegated - 3 balls
Bulky Weight Novelty Eyelash Yarn
   [1³/₄ ounces, 60 yards (50
   grams, 54 meters) per ball]:
   Blue - 1 ball
Crochet hook, size K (6.5 mm) **or**
   size needed for gauge
Yarn needle

Gauge Swatch: 4¹/₂" (11.5 cm) square
Work same as Body for 5 rows.

Body
With Variegated, ch 13.

Row 1 (Right side): Dc in fourth ch from hook **(3 skipped chs count as first dc)**, ★ ch 1, skip next ch, dc in next 2 chs; repeat from ★ 2 times **more**: 8 dc and 3 ch-1 sps.

Note: Loop a short piece of yarn around any stitch to mark Row 1 as **right** side.

Row 2: Ch 3 **(counts as first dc)**, turn; dc in next dc, (ch 1, dc in next 2 dc) across.

Repeat Row 2 for pattern until Body measures approximately 65" (165 cm) from beginning ch; finish off.

Weaving
Thread yarn needle with Blue.

Beginning at Row 1, weave Blue through ch-1 sps to last row, being careful not to pull too tightly.

Leaving an 8" (20.5 cm) tail on each end, cut Blue. Tie tail around ch on each end. Repeat, weaving 3 **more** strands through same sps; then, weave 4 strands of Blue through remaining ch-1 sps on Body in same manner.

Fringe
Cut a piece of cardboard 3" (7.5 cm) wide by 9" (23 mm) long. Wind the Blue **loosely** and **evenly** lengthwise around the cardboard until the card is filled; then, cut across one end. Repeat as needed.
Holding 3 strands of Blue together, fold in half.
With **wrong** side facing and using a crochet hook, draw the folded end up through a stitch, or space and pull the loose ends through the folded end; draw the knot up **tightly**. Repeat spacing evenly across short edges of Scarf.
Lay flat on a hard surface and trim the ends.

CD HOLDER

- 8¹/₂"x11" sheet of blue cardstock
- snowflake and snowflake border stamps
- white ink pad
- clear embossing powder
- embossing heat tool
- bleach pen
- white thread
- blue embroidery floss
- CD with recipient's favorite songs
- iridescent vellum
- vellum tape
- ³/₄" dia. blue button
- adhesive foam dots
- ¹/₈" dia. silver brads
- white handmade paper
- craft glue
- snowflake charms

1. For the holder, tear a 6¹/₈"x11" piece from cardstock. Stamp a snowflake border along one short edge on one side. While the ink is wet, sprinkle it with embossing powder. Shake off the excess powder. Follow the manufacturer's instructions to heat the powder with the embossing tool.

2. Stamp snowflakes and make dots with the bleach pen on the same side of the holder. Emboss some of the snowflakes if desired.

3. For the pocket, fold the end opposite the snowflake border 3¹/₄" to the wrong side. Sew along the long edges of the holder, securing the pocket. Fold the bordered end 2³/₄" to the wrong side for the flap. Knotting one end

on the inside, stitch a 6" floss length through the center of the flap, ¹/₂" from the end.

4. Print the CD's song titles on vellum, tear it into a 2¹/₈"x4⁵/₈" piece and tape it to the inside of the flap. Stitch the button with floss and use a foam dot to attach it to the center of the pocket, 1¹/₄" from the top edge. Place the CD in the pocket and wrap the floss around the button to keep the holder closed.

5. Print a label on vellum and tear it into a 1¹/₄"x1³/₄" piece. Use brads to attach the label to a torn handmade paper piece and glue it to the flap. Use pieces of foam dots to attach charms to the flap.

NECK WARMER

- tracing paper
- ½ yard muslin
- funnel
- 3 lbs. uncooked rice
- white bath towel
- die-cutting tool and alphabet dies
- navy felt and thread
- 7" length of ⁵⁄₈"w hook-and-loop fastener
- blue cardstock
- snowman stamp
- white ink pad
- white pencil
- craft glue
- blue printed scrapbook paper
- ⅛" dia. hole punch
- assorted fibers
- safety pin

Yardage is based on fabric with a 40" usable width.

For the rice bag, use a photocopier to enlarge the pattern on page 148 to 144%. Following *Making Patterns* on page 140 and excluding the tab, use the enlarged pattern and cut two bag pieces from muslin.

Matching the wrong sides, using a ½" seam allowance and leaving a 1" opening, zigzag the pieces together. Use the funnel to fill the bag with rice and sew the opening closed. Trim the seam allowance to ¼".

For the cover, use the enlarged pattern and cut two cover pieces (with tabs) from the towel. For the back, cut away ¾" of the top tab edge of one piece. For the front, die-cut the recipient's initials from felt. *Whipstitch* (page 140) the pieces to the cover front as shown.

Matching the right sides, using a ¼" seam allowance and leaving the tab edges open, sew the cover pieces together. Turn right side out. Sew one half of the fastener to the outer top tab edge of the cover back and the other half to the inner top tab edge of the cover front. Insert the rice bag in the cover and secure the tabs with the fastener.

Cut a 2⅛"x3⅞" cardstock tag. Stamp the snowman on the tag. Use the pencil to add names, snowflakes, "Microwave 2-4 Minutes" and a message on the tag. Glue the tag to scrapbook paper and cut the paper slightly larger than the tag. Punch a hole in the top of the tag. Knot fibers on the safety pin and use it to attach the tag to the cover.

A good book should leave you... slightly exhausted at the end. You live several lives while reading it. ~WILLIAM STYRON

READER'S SCARF

- 2¼" yards cream fleece
- 1 yard floral fabric

Yardage is based on fabrics with a 40" usable width.

1. For the scarf, cut a 24"x80" piece from fleece; round the corners.

2. For each pocket, cut a 9¾"x10½" fabric piece; round the corners on one end. Clipping the curves, press the bottom and side edges ½" to the wrong side. Press the top edge ½" to the wrong side twice; topstitch. Center and topstitch a pocket 2½" from each scarf end.

3. For the binding, cut a 23" fabric square. Follow *Continuous Bias Binding* on page 142 to cut a 2"x207" continuous bias strip from the fabric square.

4. Press one end and one long edge of the binding ½" to the wrong side. Beginning with the pressed end and matching the long raw edges, place the right side of the binding on the wrong side of the scarf. Using a ¼" seam allowance and overlapping the pressed end with the raw end, sew the unpressed edge of the binding to the wrong side of the scarf.

5. Wrap the pressed binding edge to the front; pin and topstitch.

For a doubly delightful present, tuck a new book inside the Reader's Scarf.

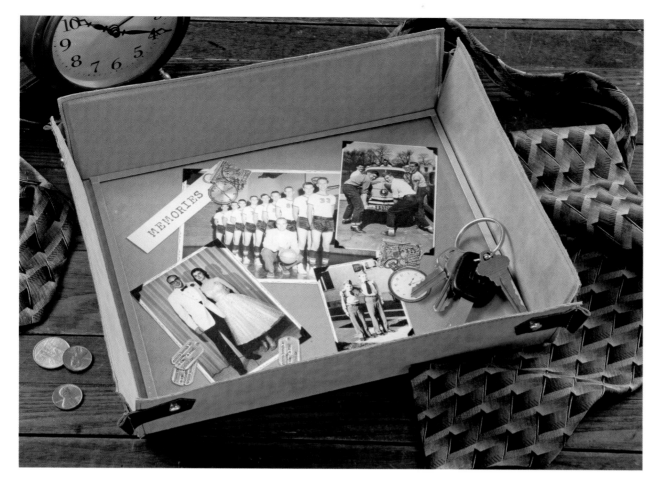

VALET TRAY

- mat board
- fusible stabilizer
- two 15¼"x17¼" pieces of camel faux suede
- spray adhesive
- dark brown faux leather
- 5/16" dia. silver studs
- craft glue
- clothespins
- 8"x10" piece of glass from a photo frame
- ½"w silver foil tape
- photos and paper memorabilia

Use spray adhesive in a well-ventilated area. Allow adhesive to dry after each application.

1. Cut two 2½"x8", two 2½"x10" and one 8"x10" piece from mat board. Fuse stabilizer to the wrong side of each suede piece. Leaving ⅛" between pieces and securing with spray adhesive, arrange the mat board pieces on the wrong side of one suede piece as shown in Fig. 1.

Fig. 1

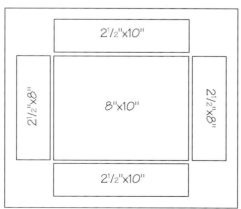

	2½"x10"	
2½"x8"	8"x10"	2½"x8"
	2½"x10"	

2. Adhere the remaining suede piece to the remaining side of the mat board, tucking the suede between the pieces. Machine sew along the creases between the mat board pieces and around the outer edges close to the mat board. Cut away the excess suede.

3. Cut four 1"x4" leather strips. Trim each end into a point; attach studs at the ends. Fold each strip in half. Starting ⅜" from the fold and working toward the fold, sew a diagonal line across the strip.

4. Fold the tray sides up and glue a strip to each corner as shown. Secure the strips with clothespins until the glue dries.

5. Cover the glass edges with foil tape. Place photos and memorabilia, then the glass in the tray.

"Laughter is the closest distance between two people."

—Victor Borge

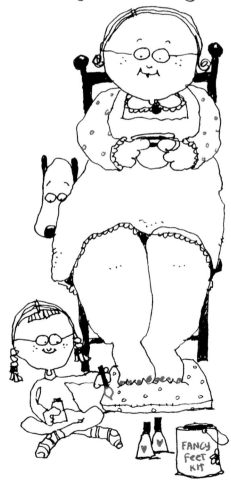

Take a load off,
hoist your feet
for a treat
that can't be beat:

No socks, no shoes
let's paint your
toesies
~ pinkies green
& big toes rosey!

PEDICURE KIT

- deckle-edged craft scissors
- assorted cardstock and scrapbook papers
- brown alphabet rub-ons
- brown gel pen
- small and large flower punches
- 1/2" dia. circle punch
- brown ink pad
- double-sided tape
- new pint-size paint can with lid
- mini pedicure set and nail polish
- 5/8 yard of 5/8"w polka-dot grosgrain ribbon
- tracing paper
- 1/8" dia. hole punch
- blue cording

For the label, use the craft scissors to cut a 2 3/4"x4" piece of cardstock. Use rub-ons to spell "fancy feet kit" on the label. Draw a border on the label 1/4" from the edges.

Punch flowers from scrapbook papers and circles from cardstock and scrapbook paper. Ink the edges of the flowers, circles and label. Tape the flowers and circles to the label and the label to the can. Tape a scrapbook paper circle to the lid.

Place the pedicure set and polish in the can. Tie ribbon around the can. Using the pattern on page 148, cut a scrapbook paper tag. Tape the tag to cardstock and cut the cardstock slightly larger than the tag. Punch a hole in the top of the tag and add "pamper!" with rub-ons. Tie the tag onto the ribbon with the cording.

When making Pedicure Kits, remember to make one for yourself. After a long day of shopping, your feet will deserve a little pampering!

GIRL'S FLEECE CAPELET

- 1¼ yards of 60"w pink fleece
- string
- fabric marking pen
- thumbtack
- ½ yard of 60"w dark pink fleece
- pencil with eraser
- tracing paper
- scrap of green fleece
- pink and green embroidery floss
- 4 yards pink and green pom-pom fringe with a ⅝"w flange

Our capelet measures 16¼" from the collar to the bottom edge. You may need to adjust the measurements of your capelet to fit your child. Use a ½" seam allowance for all sewing.

1. Cut a 41" pink fleece square. Follow *Making a Fabric Circle* on page 142 and use a 20" string measurement for the outer cutting line. Remove the tack and use a 2½" string measurement for the inner cutting line.

2. Cut through all layers along the drawn lines. For the front opening, cut through one layer along one folded edge from the outer to the inner edge; unfold. Pin the front opening edges ¾" to the wrong side and topstitch.

3. Enlarge the collar pattern on page 152 to 126%. Following *Making Patterns* on page 140, cut 2 collars from dark pink fleece. Matching the right sides and leaving the neck edge open, sew the collar pieces together. Clip the curves. Turn the collar right side out and topstitch ¼" from the seam.

4. Pin the raw edge of the collar to the wrong side of the capelet. Sew the collar to the capelet; clip the curves. Turn the capelet and collar right side out. Topstitch ¼" from the neck seam.

5. For each tie, cut a 2½"x17" strip from dark pink fleece. Matching the right sides and long edges, sew along the long edges. Trim the seam allowance to ¼". Use the eraser end of the pencil to help turn the tie right side out.

6. For each pom-pom, cut forty ½"x3" strips and one ½"x8" strip from dark pink fleece. Stack the short strips and tightly tie the long strip around the middle. Tack a pom-pom to the end of each tie. Tack the remaining tie ends to the capelet front under the collar.

7. Using the patterns on page 152, cut a dark pink fleece flower and a green fleece center. *Blanket Stitch* (page 140) the center to the flower with 3 strands of pink floss, then the flower to the capelet with 3 strands of green floss.

8. Folding the flange ends ½" to the wrong side and aligning the top of the flange with the bottom raw edge of the capelet, pin the fringe to the right side of the capelet. Zigzag along the bottom edge of the flange. Fold the bottom edge of the capelet ¾" to the wrong side and topstitch.

Peace begins with a Smile.
- Mother Teresa

BEST GRANNY

SNOWMAN PILLOW WITH JAMMIE BAG HAT

- ⁵⁄₈ yard of 60"w white plush fleece
- string
- fabric marking pen
- thumbtack
- orange and black felt scraps
- orange, black and blue embroidery floss
- 1" dia. black flower buttons
- pink chalk or blush and applicator
- polyester fiberfill
- ¹⁄₂ yard of ultra-soft 60"w blue dotted fleece
- ¹⁄₂" dia. white pom-poms
- fabric glue
- 28" length of red jumbo chenille rickrack

Use a ¹⁄₂" seam allowance for all sewing.

Cut two 17" squares from white fleece. Follow *Making a Fabric Circle* on page 142 and use a 7¹⁄₂" string measurement to cut a 15" circle from each square for the pillow front and back.

Cut a nose and mouth from felt. Using 6 strands of floss, sew the buttons to the pillow front for the eyes. *Blanket Stitch* (page 140) the nose and *Whipstitch* the mouth to the pillow front. Blush the cheeks.

Matching the right sides and leaving an opening for turning, sew the pillow front and back together.

Turn the pillow right side out, stuff it and sew the opening closed.

For the hat, cut a 15"x29" blue fleece piece. Matching the right sides, sew the short edges together and turn right side out. Sew a 1" hem along one end for the bottom. Leaving the back open for the jammie bag, tack the bottom edge of the hat to the pillow front only. Sew *Running Stitches* 2" from the top of the hat. Pull the thread tight, wrap it around the gathers three times and knot to secure. Make ¹⁄₄"w cuts in the top edge for fringe. Randomly sew pom-poms to the fringe. Glue rickrack along the bottom edge of the hat.

REINDEER TOWEL & BATH MITT

- two 16"x30" tan hand towels and a 30"x56" tan bath towel
- tan, brown, black and white thread
- tracing paper
- brown, black and white felt
- polyester fiberfill
- Sizzix® die-cutting tool and upper and lower case "O" dies
- fabric glue
- 1" and ³/₄" dia. red pom-poms

Match the right sides and use a ¹/₂" seam allowance unless otherwise indicated.

TOWEL

1. Using a photocopier, enlarge the hood pattern on page 153 to 150% and cut it out. Fold one hand towel in half, matching the short edges. Aligning the bottom edge of the pattern with the short edges of the towel, use the enlarged pattern to cut 2 hood pieces from the folded towel.

2. Leaving the bottom and front edges open, sew the hood pieces together. Fold the front edge ¹/₂" to the wrong side twice and topstitch. Turn the hood right side out.

3. Using the patterns on page 152, cut 4 ears from the hand towel scraps and 4 antlers (2 in reverse) from brown felt. Leaving the bottom edges open, sew the ears together in pairs; turn right side out. Pinching the bottom of the ears to pleat, *Whipstitch (page 140)* the ears to the hood as shown.

4. Matching the wrong sides and using a ¹/₄" seam allowance, sew the antlers together in pairs; do not turn. Trim the seam allowance to ¹/₈". Stuff the antlers. *Whipstitch* the antlers to the hood behind the ears.

5. For each eye, use the upper case die to cut an "O" from black and white felt. Using the outlines from the white die-cuts and the centers from the black die-cuts, glue the eyes to the hood as shown. Tack the 1" pom-pom to the hood for the nose.

6. Center and sew the bottom edge of the hood on one long edge of the bath towel.

(continued on page 138)

Several years ago, I was watching my nieces and nephews open many, many gifts. Although elated to see the joy in their faces, it saddened me to think of others not even having one brightly wrapped package. The next year was to be different. Each child received a gift especially for him or her, but instead of gifts on end, there was also a check to be donated to a charity of the child's choice. For example, one nephew loves to eat so he was given gift certificates to some of his favorite food chains…he, in turn, used his other half of the gift to feed a dozen homeless men a turkey dinner at our local shelter. An animal-loving niece received a large stuffed animal because she chose to send her gift to Animal Friends. It has expanded to the adults. Our family gardener was given new gloves and a few tools while crops were planted in Guatemala in her name. It is fun and feels so good (twice!). It is always better to give than to receive.

—Karen Petrie

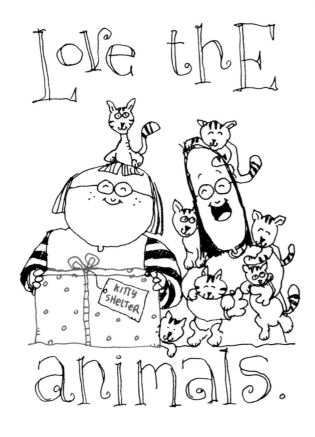

PET ALBUMS

- freezer paper
- wool felt for the background and in colors to match your pet
- coordinating embroidery floss
- pinking shears
- polyester fiberfill
- 1/8" dia. hole punch
- assorted ribbons and trims
- fabric glue
- spiral-bound album
- brads

For the Cat Album:
- jingle bell

For the Dog Album:
- two 5/8" dia. brown buttons
- leather watchband
- cardstock
- alphabet rub-ons
- clear dimensional glaze
- 1/16" dia. hole punch
- jump ring

CAT ALBUM

1. For the appliqués, trace the cat patterns on page 154 onto the dull side of the freezer paper; cut them out. Iron the shiny side of the patterns to the wrong side of the desired wool colors; cut them out. Cut wool "spots" as desired.

2. Leaving a tail, wrap floss around the ball for yarn. Layer the pieces on a pinked felt background cut to fit on the album cover. *Blanket Stitch* (page 140) the pieces in place with 3 strands of floss, lightly stuffing as you sew. Add *Straight Stitch* details as desired.

3. For the collar, punch a 1/8" hole in the background on each side of the cat's neck. Thread the bell onto the center of a 4" ribbon length. Thread the ribbon through the holes and knot at the back.

4. Glue the appliquéd background to the front album cover. Punch 1/8" holes through both layers at the background corners. Attach brads through the holes. Knot ribbon and trim around the binding.

DOG ALBUM

1. Using the dog patterns on page 154, follow Step 1 of the Cat Album.

2. Layer the pieces (except the nose and mouth) on the center of a pinked felt background cut to fit on the album cover. *Blanket Stitch* (page 140) the pieces in place with 3 strands of floss, lightly stuffing as you sew. Add *Straight Stitch* details as desired.

3. Glue the nose and mouth in place. Sew the buttons to the face for the eyes.

4. For the collar, cut the buckled watchband to fit across the dog's neck. Cut a bone from cardstock. Use rub-ons to spell "rruff" on the bone. Apply glaze to the bone and allow to dry. Punch a 1/16" hole in the bone and attach it to the collar with the jump ring. Glue the collar in place.

5. Follow Step 4 of the Cat Album.

SANTA DOORMAT

- red and green felt
- tracing paper
- dark brown wool
- fabric glue
- dark brown embroidery floss
- chenille doormat
- green jumbo rickrack

Use a computer to print "Santa's Been Here." Enlarge the letters to the desired size with a photocopier. Using the enlarged letters as a pattern, cut felt letters. Using the patterns on page 146, cut wool footprints. Glue the letters and use floss to sew the footprints to the mat as shown. Layer and glue rickrack and red felt strips along the short edges of the mat.

Gifts in the Nick of time

*Christmas is the season
for sharing! As your gift list grows,
it's sometimes difficult to think of things
to give everyone. Rather than making a
different gift for each person, make several of
the same gift. Everyone could use a Christmas
Address Book to make sending cards a snap,
while a manicure set or handmade earrings are
just right for all your friends. So pick a
gift and get started crafting...Christmas
will be here soon!*

*Who wouldn't love a new manicure set for Christmas? Add a playful
touch to a purchased set by painting the pieces with whimsical dots
and stripes. A white candy box tied with polka-dot ribbon makes a
perfect presentation. See page 138 to make this gift in a flash!*

CHRISTMAS ADDRESS BOOK

You'll remember everyone on your Christmas card list with this Christmas Address Book. Glue a scrapbook paper cover to a journal. Apply a large "C" sticker to a wavy-edged green cardstock square; then, sew the green square to a torn red cardstock square, leaving long thread ends. Glue the square to the front cover and use rub-ons to finish spelling "Christmas" on the cover. Tack red jute to the end of the page marker and tie jingle bells onto the ends. Use rub-ons to spell "address book" on a ribbon length. Tie the ribbon around the book to keep it closed.

Need a quick but festive way to wrap a two-part gift? See page 139 to make a Penny Sack and matching Gift Box (below).

In the early 1800's, it was a tradition to send holiday letters to friends and relatives who lived far away. But in 1843, an Englishman named Henry Cole was too busy to write his usual letters, so he hired John C. Horsley, an artist, to design an illustrated card. The card featured three panels...the middle was a scene of a celebrating family, while the two side panels represented acts of Christmas charity. Before long, the tradition of sending Christmas cards began!

above the 2" cardstock square. Punch another hole 1" above the first. Attach the rivet through the top hole. For the tag, write a message on a $1/2$"x$3/4$" cardstock piece and sandwich it between the clear adhesive tags. Knot the snowflake ornament and tag onto the center of the brown ribbon. Thread one ribbon end through the bottom hole to the inside front, then through the rivet to the outside front. Tie a bow on the card front.

Treat your friends to a pair of handmade earrings! Instructions for crafting the earrings and jolly gift tag are on page 139.

GIFT CARDS

- craft glue
- green striped and mauve and cream polka-dot scrapbook papers
- cream cardstock
- brown ink pad
- black fine-point permanent pen
- black alphabet rub-ons
- brown and cream thread
- $1/8$" and $1/4$" dia. hole punches
- double-sided tape
- candy cane
- $5/8$ yard of $1/4$"w cream silk ribbon
- hot glue gun
- cream buttons
- snap-on scrapbooking rivet
- two $5/8$"x1" clear adhesive tags
- 2" snowflake ornament
- $3/8$ yard of $1/8$"w brown ribbon

CANDY CANE CARD

Glue a 4"x$5 5/8$" striped paper piece to a $4 1/4$"x6" cardstock piece; then, gluing only at the center, glue two 2"x3" pieces of polka-dot paper to the striped paper as shown. Ink the card as desired and use the pen and rub-ons to add a message. Zigzag along all the paper edges with brown thread. Punch two $1/4$" diameter holes, $1 1/2$" apart, in the center of the card. Tape the candy cane to the card between the holes. Thread silk ribbon through the holes from back to front and knot the ends at the front around the candy cane. Knot a few extra ribbon lengths around the first and hot glue buttons, threaded with cream thread, over the knots.

SNOWFLAKE CARD

Matching the short edges, fold a 5"x10" cardstock piece in half. Gluing only at the centers, adhere a $4 5/8$" polka-dot paper square to the center of the card front and a 2" cardstock square near the bottom of the polka-dot square. Ink the card as desired. Zigzag along the edges of the squares on the front with brown thread. Glue a 5" cardstock square to the inside card front. Punch a $1/8$" diameter hole in the card front just

card. Use a brad to attach a charm to the snowflake paper and glue the paper to the card front.

For the label, cut a 1³/₄"x2" green cardstock square with craft scissors and glue it to a 2"x2¹/₈" handwriting paper piece. Zigzag along the left edge with brown thread. Add a message on the label. Use a brad to attach a charm to the label and glue it to the card back. Wrap ribbon around the card as shown, knotting and trimming the ends at the front.

Punch two green cardstock circles. Attach a circle and charm to the envelope flap with a brad. Close the flap and attach a circle to the envelope, just below the flap, with a brad. Wrap jute around the brads to close the envelope.

CHRISTMAS ATC

Artist Trading Cards, or ATCs, are a popular way to exhibit scrapbooking skills on a smaller scale. The cards are made by decorating 2¹/₂"x3¹/₂" playing cards. You can display your completed cards or trade them with other scrapbook enthusiasts. Check on the Internet or at your local scrapbook store to join in the trading fun. Follow our easy suggestions and use your imagination and favorite scrapbook embellishments to make each card.

- craft glue
- 2¹/₂"x3¹/₂" playing card
- red and green cardstock
- snowman and Christmas greeting ephemera
- deckle-edged craft scissors
- snowflake and handwriting scrapbook papers
- silver brads
- silver snowflake charms
- brown thread
- alphabet and date stamps
- brown ink pad
- black fine-point permanent pen
- 12" length of ¹/₄"w red ribbon
- 3"x4" white vellum envelope
- ³/₄" dia. circle punch
- jute

Cover the card face with red cardstock. Trim the ephemera edges with craft scissors. Mat the snowman ephemera with red cardstock and glue it and the greeting to a snowflake paper piece slightly smaller than the

An original is hard to find but easy to recognize.

- JOHN MASON -

ATC ALBUM WITH CARD

- 22"x28" cream cardstock sheet
- stylus
- clear plastic sheets
- brown thread
- 1/8" dia. eyelets
- eyelet setter
- red and brown cardstock
- assorted hole and shape punches
- craft glue
- alphabet stamps
- brown ink pad
- light blue scrapbook paper
- 21" length of 1/2"w brown rickrack
- tracing paper
- red embroidery floss
- 2 1/2"x3 1/2" playing card
- Christmas ephemera

1. For the album, cut a 6"x28" cream cardstock piece. Mark seven 4" wide sections on the cardstock. Use the stylus to score the back or front of the album as indicated in Fig. 1. Referring to the photo, accordion-fold the album.

Fig. 1

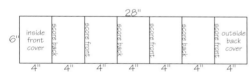

Looking for an ideal gift for your scrapbooking friends? Give them ATC Albums so they'll have a clever way to store and display their Artist Trading Cards.

2. For the pockets, cut five 2 1/2"x3" plastic pieces. Center a plastic piece, 1" from the bottom, on each inside album section. Sew the pockets to the album along the side and bottom edges. Attach eyelets at the top corners of each pocket.

3. Cut a 3 1/2"x5 1/4" red cardstock rectangle. Punch shapes from the rectangle and glue it to the album front. Glue the punched shapes to the album as desired. Stamp "A.T.C." onto a 3/4"x2 1/4" scrapbook paper piece. Trim a punched shape and glue it to the paper. Layer and glue a 7/8"x2 1/2" brown cardstock piece and the scrapbook paper piece on the album front.

4. Close the album. Center and glue the rickrack across the back cover; tie the ends into a bow at the front. Cut a tag from brown cardstock. Stamp "for you!" on a small scrapbook paper piece and glue it to the tag. Punch a hole in the top of the tag and tie it onto the rickrack with floss.

5. For the card inside the album, cover the playing card with brown cardstock. Layer and glue cream cardstock and red punched cardstock on the brown cardstock. Glue Christmas ephemera to the card.

First ponder, then DARE.
-HELMUTH VON MOLTKE

S'MORE BARS PACKAGE

- 12"x12" sheets of brown and cream cardstock
- brown chalk
- craft glue
- brown thread
- 1 yard of 1½"w green satin ribbon
- ⅜ yard each of 1"w cream and ⅜"w pink satin ribbons
- black alphabet rub-ons
- white vellum
- deckle-edged and scallop-edged craft scissors
- ⅛" square silver brads
- sandpaper
- pink striped and pink floral print scrapbook paper
- ⅜" dia. grommet and grommet kit
- 6¼" length of ¼"w brown velvet ribbon
- Kelly's S'more Bars
- cellophane bag
- twist tie
- ⅝ yard each of ¼"w green, pink and cream silk ribbons
- tracing paper
- alphabet stamps
- brown ink pad
- ⅛" dia. hole punch
- adhesive foam dot

1. Tear away ½" of each long edge of a 7"x12" brown cardstock piece. With the short edges at the top, fold the cardstock into three 4" sections for the package.

2. Chalk the edges of a 3¾"x5½" cream cardstock piece. Gluing at the center only, attach the cardstock to the package front and sew along the edges in a random pattern.

3. Machine sew decorative stitches along one long edge of a 13" green satin ribbon length. Layer and glue the green ribbon and a 13" length each of cream and pink satin ribbon down the front of the package, wrapping the ends to the wrong side. Use rub-ons to spell "s'more bars" on vellum; trim to 1¼"x2" with deckle-edged scissors. Use brads to attach the vellum to the package front.

4. For the top flap, sand a 5"x6¼" striped paper piece and fold it in half, matching the long edges. Cut a 1"x6¼" floral print paper strip and trim away ¼" of one long edge with scallop-edged scissors. Glue the strip to the back of the flap along one long edge for the front. Attach the grommet to the center front of the flap, 1" from the fold. Glue the velvet ribbon along the front edge of the flap. Overlapping ⅝" of the top back edge of the package, zigzag the back edge of the flap to the package.

5. Place S'more Bars in the bag and close with the twist tie. Tie a 22" green satin ribbon length into a bow around the top of the bag. Place the bag in the package. Loop a 22" length of each silk ribbon around the bow, thread the ends through the grommet and tie into a bow at the front to close the package.

6. Using the pattern on page 143, cut a floral print paper tag and stamp it with a message. Chalk the edges and punch a hole in the top. Tie one silk ribbon end to the tag and secure it on the package with the foam dot.

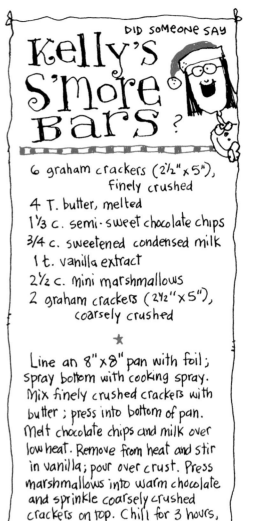

DID SOMEONE SAY

Kelly's S'more Bars?

6 graham crackers (2½"x5"), finely crushed
4 T. butter, melted
1⅓ c. semi-sweet chocolate chips
¾ c. sweetened condensed milk
1 t. vanilla extract
2½ c. mini marshmallows
2 graham crackers (2½"x5"), coarsely crushed

★

Line an 8"x8" pan with foil; spray bottom with cooking spray. Mix finely crushed crackers with butter; press into bottom of pan. Melt chocolate chips and milk over low heat. Remove from heat and stir in vanilla; pour over crust. Press marshmallows into warm chocolate and sprinkle coarsely crushed crackers on top. Chill for 3 hours, remove foil and cut into bars.
—Makes 32 bars.—

Glue a stamped round cardstock label to the tag. Punch a hole through the tag and tie it to the bag with jute. Fill the pot with excelsior and place the bag inside. Place the pot in the box and fill in with ornaments and berries. Wrap ribbons around the box and tie into a bow at the front.

Offering the promise of spring in the middle of winter, the paperwhite narcissus is one of the easiest bulbs to force into bloom in your home. Paperwhite Kits are an ideal gift for co-workers, your garden club, or your book club. Other bulbs that will work are amaryllis and hyacinth. What a nice way for anyone to add color or fragrance to their days!

PAPERWHITE KIT
- 4³/₄"x4³/₄"x6" papier-mâché box
- ceiling tin paintable wallpaper
- greenery
- scallop-edged craft scissors
- small brown paper bag
- paperwhite bulbs
- ¹/₃ yard each of ¹/₄"w green-checked and ¹/₈"w blue-green ribbons
- red jute
- craft glue
- alphabet and leaf stamps
- brown ink pad
- 1³/₄" dia. circle punch
- green cardstock
- 2" dia. metal-rimmed tag
- ¹/₈" dia. hole punch
- 4³/₈" dia.x3¹/₈" tall clay pot
- wood excelsior
- vintage ornaments
- tallow berries
- 1 yard each of ⁷/₈"w red and ³/₈"w blue-green ribbons

Cover the box with wallpaper and fill with greenery. Trim the top of the bag with craft scissors. Place the bulbs in the bag and tie ribbon and jute into a bow around the top.

Kitchen Creations to Share

If you're like Kate, Holly and
Mary Elizabeth, Christmastime most likely
finds you in the kitchen. So why not combine two
of your favorite holiday activities…cooking and giving?
We've filled this section with flavor-packed presents
that are as much fun to make as they are to share.
And for an extra-special touch, offer your
goodies in handcrafted gift containers!

Please a passel of palates with this assortment of
edible offerings…Marshmallow Pops, Traditional Party Mix,
Initial Cookies, Buckeyes, Jambalaya Mix and Creamy Potato Soup
Mix. Whether you need snacks for your child's class party
or a gift for your co-workers, we've got just the recipe!

SWEETEN UP YOUR COFFEE OR COCOA!

the Sweetest SPOONS

1 c. CHOCOLATE CHIPS
1 c. BUTTERSCOTCH CHIPS
16 TO 20 PLASTIC SPOONS
OPTIONAL: COLORFUL SPRINKLES

PLACE ½ CUP CHOCOLATE CHIPS IN A MICROWAVE-SAFE BOWL; HEAT IN MICROWAVE IN 30-SECOND INTERVALS, STIRRING AFTER EACH INTERVAL, 'TIL MELTED & SMOOTH. USING HALF THE SPOONS, DIP IN THE MELTED CHOCOLATE TO COVER BOWL OF THE SPOON. PLACE ON WAX PAPER ON A BAKING SHEET. REPEAT MELTING & DIPPING PROCESS IN A SEPARATE BOWL WITH REMAINING SPOONS & ½ CUP BUTTERSCOTCH CHIPS. PLACE SPOONS ON WAX PAPER; CHILL 'TIL FIRM. ONCE HARDENED, MELT THE REMAINING ½ CUP CHOCOLATE CHIPS & BUTTERSCOTCH CHIPS IN SEPARATE BOWLS. DIP THE CHOCOLATE-COVERED SPOONS INTO THE MELTED BUTTERSCOTCH CHIPS, AND DIP THE BUTTERSCOTCH-COVERED SPOONS IN THE MELTED CHOCOLATE CHIPS; PLACE ON WAX PAPER. SPRINKLE WITH COLORFUL SPRINKLES, IF DESIRED. CHILL 'TIL FIRM BEFORE WRAPPING INDIVIDUALLY. MAKES 1½ DOZEN.

The Sweetest Spoons

FELT COASTER & TAG

For the coaster, use Cross Stitches (page 140) and 3 strands of white embroidery floss to sew a 4¼" green felt square to a 4¾" scallop-edged red felt square.

For the tag, use the patterns on page 157 to cut a small tag from textured red cardstock, a large tag from white cardstock and a tree from green felt. Zigzag the tree on the small tag with white thread and add "for you!" with alphabet rub-ons. Glue the small tag to the large tag and punch a hole in the top.

Fill a mug with coffee beans. Arrange The Sweetest Spoons in the beans. Place the coaster on a 4½" cardboard square. Place the mug on the coaster. Wrap the gift with cellophane and close with a twist tie. Knot ribbon around the top. Attach the tag with red jute.

MARSHMALLOW COCOA MIX

This quick & easy cocoa is a favorite for kids of all ages.

25-oz. pkg. powdered milk
1½ c. powdered non-dairy creamer
3 c. hot cocoa mix
1½ c. powdered sugar
2 c. mini marshmallows

Combine all ingredients; equally divide into four, one-quart jars. Attach gift tag with instructions to each jar. Makes 4 jars.

Instructions: Combine ½ cup mix with one cup boiling water. Makes one serving.

Write the lyrics to a favorite Christmas carol on a solid color mug using glass paint and then tuck in a package of Marshmallow Cocoa Mix…a simple, one-of-a-kind gift!

WARM SIPS SPICE BUNDLES

Delightful after a day of fun in the snow.

8 cinnamon sticks, crushed
2 whole nutmegs, grated
1/3 c. whole cloves
2 T. orange zest
2 T. lemon zest
1/4 c. whole allspice
cheesecloth

Combine ingredients in a mixing bowl. Place one tablespoon mixture in the center of a double-thickness 4"x4" square of cheesecloth and tie closed; repeat with remaining mixture. Store in an airtight container before giving; attach instructions. Makes about 15 bundles.

Instructions: Simmer one quart cider or tea with one spice bundle in a large saucepan. Ladle into mugs. Makes 4 servings.

MALT CHOCOLATE WAFFLE MIX

A warm and tasty breakfast mix that is handy to have waiting in the pantry all winter long.

2 1/2 c. buttermilk biscuit baking mix
1/3 c. powdered malted milk
1/3 c. mini chocolate chips
2 T. sugar

Combine all ingredients in a large plastic zipping bag; seal. Attach instructions.

Instructions: Place mix in a large mixing bowl; set aside. Beat 2 egg whites until stiff peaks form; set aside. Add 2 egg yolks, 1 1/3 cups buttermilk and 1/2 cup melted butter to mix; blend well. Fold in egg whites; heat according to waffle iron manufacturer's instructions. Makes 6 servings.

GIFT OF THE MAGI BREAD

Make several loaves to give to your neighbors.

1/2 c. butter or margarine, softened
1 c. sugar
2 eggs
1 t. vanilla extract
2 c. all-purpose flour
1 t. baking soda
1/8 t. salt
1 c. mashed bananas
11-oz. can mandarin orange segments, drained
6-oz. pkg. chocolate chips
1 c. shredded coconut
1/2 c. sliced almonds or chopped walnuts or pecans
1/2 c. chopped maraschino cherries

Combine butter or margarine with sugar. Add eggs and vanilla; beat until fluffy. Combine flour, baking soda and salt. Add flour mixture and bananas alternately to the sugar mixture. Stir in orange segments, chocolate chips, coconut, nuts and cherries. Pour into 2 greased loaf pans. Bake at 350 degrees for 1 to 1 1/4 hours. Makes 2 loaves.

Pat Milliman

OLD-FASHIONED APPLE BUTTER

By using applesauce, you don't even need to peel apples!

1 gal. applesauce
4 1/2 c. sugar
2 t. cinnamon
1 t. ground cloves
half-pint canning jars and lids, sterilized

Combine all ingredients in a large mixing bowl. Pour into a 6-quart slow cooker. Cook, uncovered, on low for 8 to 12 hours, stirring occasionally. After cooking, check the thickness. If apple butter is too thin, continue cooking until it reaches desired thickness. Fill sterilized pint jars, clean rims and place lids and rings on, securing tightly. Process in a boiling water bath for 20 minutes. Remove jars from water; lids should pull down as jars cool. Makes 7 to 9 pints.

Linda Smeiles
Kent, OH

"Get not your friends by bare compliments, but by giving them sensible tokens of your love."
— Socrates

Holiday cranberry Jam ...good on toast!

2 c. CRANBERRIES
1 ORANGE, PEELED & DIVIDED INTO SECTIONS
16-OZ. PKG. FROZEN STRAWBERRIES, THAWED
3 C. SUGAR
3 OZ. LIQUID FRUIT PECTIN
5 HALF-PINT CANNING JARS & LIDS, STERILIZED

COARSELY GRIND CRANBERRIES & ORANGE SECTIONS IN A FOOD PROCESSOR; SPOON INTO A HEAVY STOCKPOT. ADD STRAWBERRIES & SUGAR. BRING MIXTURE TO A FULL ROLLING BOIL OVER HIGH HEAT, STIRRING CONSTANTLY FOR ONE MINUTE. REMOVE FROM HEAT AND STIR IN PECTIN. SKIM OFF ANY FOAM and IMMEDIATELY POUR INTO HOT, STERILIZED JARS; SECURE LIDS. PROCESS JARS IN A BOILING WATER BATH FOR 10 MINUTES. MAKES 5 JARS.

↪ A RECIPE FROM
Donna Reid ★
Payson, AZ

TAG AND CARD DECK COVER

- brown and textured green cardstock
- ¼" dia. hole punch
- brown fine-point permanent pen
- brown ink pad
- deck of 2½"x3½" playing cards and an extra Queen of Hearts and Joker card
- craft knife and cutting mat
- ruler
- alphabet rub-ons and beads
- craft glue
- cellophane bag filled with Cayenne Cheddar Crackers and closed with a twist tie
- ¼"w green silk ribbon
- glue dots

For the tag, cut a 3⅛"x5" brown cardstock piece. Cut away the corners on one end and punch a hole at the top. Outline the edges of the tag and hole with the pen; then, ink the edges. Use the craft knife to cut slits in the tag for opposite corners of the extra Queen card to fit through. Tuck the corners of the card into the slits. Tear a 1"x6¾" green cardstock strip. Add a rub-on message in the center of the strip. Center the strip at an angle over the tag; glue the ends to the back. Glue beads above the card to spell "QUEEN." Tie the tag onto the cellophane bag with ribbon.

For the card deck cover, cut a 2¼"x7½" green cardstock strip and a 1⅝"x3¼" brown cardstock piece. Ink the edges. Cut out the Joker from the extra card. Attach the Joker to the brown piece and the brown piece to the center of the green strip with glue dots. Use rub-ons to spell "good times" on the strip as shown. Loosely wrap the strip around the deck of cards and glue the ends together at the back where they overlap.

Woo·eee!
Cayenne Cheddar Crackers

2 c. all-purpose flour
1 t. salt
¼ t. cayenne pepper
¼ t. dry mustard
¾ c. chilled butter
½ c. shredded cheddar cheese
6 to 8 T. cold water

...Heat 'em up even more by stirring in a few drops of hot pepper sauce or a teaspoon of diced green chiles!

Combine first 4 ingredients in a mixing bowl; cut in butter with a pastry cutter 'til coarse crumbs form. Stir in cheese and add just enough water to hold the dough together; shape into a ball and wrap in plastic wrap. Refrigerate for at least 30 minutes. Roll dough out to ⅛-inch thickness on lightly floured surface and cut out using heart, spade, club & diamond cookie cutters. Place on parchment paper-lined baking sheets; bake at 350 degrees for 10 to 12 minutes. Cool; store in airtight containers. Makes 4 dozen.

Cayenne Cheddar Crackers

Traditional Party Mix

PAPIER-MÂCHÉ BOWL

- large plastic bowl
- non-stick vegetable spray
- plastic wrap
- newspaper
- foam paintbrush
- matte decoupage glue
- red tissue paper
- white cardstock
- deckle-edged craft scissors
- alphabet stamps
- black ink pad
- 1/8" dia. hole punch
- red twine
- cellophane bags filled with Traditional Party Mix and closed with twist ties
- Christmas tea towels

1. Coat the outside of the plastic bowl with vegetable spray; then, cover it with plastic wrap.

2. Cut strips from newspaper (ours measure 3/4"x6").

3. To papier-mâché the bowl, brush glue on both sides of each strip. Overlapping the strip edges, cover the outside of the bowl. Apply 3 or 4 layers and allow to dry overnight.

4. Remove the bowl and plastic wrap from the papier-mâché bowl. Using decoupage glue and overlapping the edges of the squares, cover the bowl with 2 1/2" tissue paper squares. Allow to dry overnight.

5. Glue cardstock to a sheet of newspaper. Cut 2"x4" tags from the layered paper and cardstock. Use the craft scissors to cut a 1 1/2"x2 3/4" cardstock label. Stamp "PARTY MIX" on the label and ink the edges. Glue a torn tissue paper piece and the label on the tag. Punch a hole in the top of the tag. Use twine to tie the tags onto the cellophane bags. Arrange the towels and bags in the bowl.

TRADITIONAL PARTY MIX

Don't forget the people who deliver your mail and daily paper...they would appreciate you thinking of them during the holidays.

1/2 c. butter
2 T. Worcestershire sauce
3/4 t. garlic powder
1 1/2 t. seasoned salt
1 t. onion powder
1/2 t. celery salt
hot pepper sauce to taste
1 c. mini pretzel sticks
4 c. doughnut-shaped oat cereal
4 c. bite-size crispy wheat or bran cereal squares
4 c. bite-size crispy rice or corn cereal squares
2 c. mixed nuts

Combine the first 7 ingredients in a saucepan. Heat over low heat, stirring until butter melts; set aside. Toss remaining ingredients in a large roasting pan; pour butter mixture on top, tossing to coat. Bake at 300 degrees for 45 minutes, stirring every 15 minutes. Spread on aluminum foil to cool. Store in an airtight container. Makes 15 cups.

EASIEST CHEESE BALL

Make 'em mini...just roll into 6 small balls, wrap individually and give with some crackers.

2 8-oz. pkgs. cream cheese, softened
2 8-oz. pkgs. shredded sharp Cheddar cheese
1-oz. pkg. ranch dressing mix
1/4 t. hot pepper sauce
10-oz. pkg. chopped pecans

Combine cream cheese, Cheddar cheese, dressing mix and hot pepper sauce; form into a ball. Roll ball in chopped pecans to cover. Refrigerate overnight before serving. Makes 12 servings.

PAINT CAN

- two 19" ribbon lengths
- new pint-size paint can with lid
- scallop-edged craft scissors
- white and assorted printed scrapbook papers
- craft glue
- alphabet stickers and rub-ons
- rubber band
- black fine-point permanent pen

Tie the ribbon lengths around the center of the can. Using the craft scissors as desired, cut 3 different-sized paper ovals. Layer and glue the ovals together. Use stickers and rub-ons to spell "jambalaya mix" on the ovals. Glue the ovals to the can as shown. Stretch the rubber band over the can to secure the label; remove after the glue has dried. Cut one 2" diameter circle each from white and printed papers. Using the craft scissors as desired, cut 2 smaller circles from printed papers. Layer and glue the smaller circles on the 2" printed circle. Write "to:" and "from:" and add names on the layered circles. Glue only the top $^3/_8$" of the layered circles to the white circle. Once the glue has dried, fold the layered circles back and write the instructions for preparing the Jambalaya on the white circle. Glue the white circle to the center of the lid.

"Somehow, not only for Christmas,
But all the long year through,
The joy that you give to others
Is the joy that comes back to you."
— John Greenleaf Whittier

Jambalaya Mix

JAMBALAYA MIX!

MAKE UP SEVERAL BATCHES FOR FRIENDS WHO CRAVE CAJUN!

1 c. long-cooking rice, uncooked
1 T. dried, minced onion
1 T. green pepper flakes
1 T. dried parsley
1 bay leaf
2 t. beef bouillon granules
1/2 t. garlic powder
1/2 t. dried thyme
1/2 t. cayenne pepper

Combine all ingredients; place in a plastic zipping bag. Seal securely; attach instructions.

instructions:

COMBINE MIX WITH 3 CUPS WATER IN A LARGE STOCKPOT; BRING TO A BOIL. REDUCE HEAT; ADD 1/2 CUP DICED HAM and AN 8-OUNCE CAN OF TOMATO SAUCE. COVER and SIMMER FOR 15 TO 20 MINUTES OR UNTIL MOST OF THE LIQUID IS ABSORBED. STIR IN 1/2 CUP COOKED SHRIMP; HEAT 5 ADDITIONAL MINUTES. REMOVE FROM HEAT; DISCARD BAY LEAF BEFORE SERVING. MAKES 6 CUPS.

ABC WinterTime Soup Mix

THIS MAKES A WARM, HEARTY TREAT THAT WILL BRING CHEERS!

14-OZ. PKG. DRIED SPLIT GREEN PEAS
1-1/2 C. LONG-COOKING BROWN RICE, UNCOOKED
14-OZ. PKG. ALPHABET MACARONI
12-OZ. PKG. DRIED LENTILS
12-OZ. PKG. PEARLED BARLEY
4 C. DRIED MINCED ONION

COMBINE ALL INGREDIENTS IN A LARGE AIRTIGHT CONTAINER OR IN INDIVIDUAL 1-1/2 CUP PACKAGES. STORE IN COOL, DRY PLACE FOR UP TO 6 MONTHS. ATTACH INSTRUCTIONS. MAKES ABOUT 12 CUPS SOUP MIX.

* INSTRUCTIONS *

6 C. WATER
1-1/2 C. SOUP MIX
1-1/2 T. GARLIC SALT
2 CARROTS, SLICED
2 STALKS CELERY, SLICED
1-1/2 C. CABBAGE, SHREDDED
2 15-OZ. CANS TOMATO SAUCE
24-OZ. CAN COCKTAIL VEGETABLE JUICE
1 LB. GROUND BEEF, BROWNED

PLACE WATER, SOUP MIX and GARLIC SALT IN LARGE DUTCH OVEN; BRING TO BOIL. REDUCE HEAT; SIMMER, COVERED, FOR 1-1/2 HOURS. ADD REMAINING INGREDIENTS; SIMMER 'TIL VEGGIES ARE TENDER, ABOUT 20 MINUTES. SERVES 6 TO 8.

SOUP MUG

Fill a cellophane bag with Creamy Potato Soup Mix. Fold the bag opening to the back and tape it closed. For the bag topper, fold a 4½" diameter red cardstock circle in half. Use a black permanent pen, paper scrap, rub-ons and stickers to add the title to the front half of the topper; add red staples along the front edge (you can color plain staples with a permanent pen). Write the instructions for preparing the soup on the back half. Knot short lengths of assorted ribbons and rickrack and glue them along the fold on the topper front. Sandwich the top of the bag in the fold of the topper and secure with double-sided tape. Place the bag in a 2½-cup mug.

Cut a 1⅝"x2⅜" cardstock tag. Punch a hole in the top. Add a message with a black permanent pen, paper scrap and alphabet rub-ons. Add red staples along the edges and tie the tag onto the mug handle with rickrack.

CREAMY POTATO SOUP MIX

Be sure to give with a package of crackers or homemade bread sticks.

3½ c. instant potato flakes
3 c. powdered milk
¼ c. chicken bouillon granules
.9-oz. pkg. vegetable soup mix
2 T. dried parsley
1 t. salt
½ t. black pepper

Combine all ingredients. Store in an airtight container until ready to give. Attach instructions. Makes about 6¾ cups soup mix.

Instructions: Place one cup soup mix in a 2½-cup mug and stir in 2 cups boiling water (if using an 8-oz. mug, use ½ cup soup mix and stir in one cup boiling water). Stir until thickened, about 2 or 3 minutes. Makes one serving.

Creamy Potato Soup Mix not only makes a warm-the-spirits holiday present, it also makes an ideal get well gift any time a friend is under the weather.

Creamy Potato Soup Mix

GIFT CONES

- tracing paper
- brown and textured cream cardstock
- ¹/₈" dia. hole punch
- alphabet and assorted Christmas greeting stamps
- red and brown ink pads
- scallop-edged craft scissors
- craft glue
- ¹/₄"w green silk ribbon
- triangular cellophane bags
- Chocolate-Covered Espresso Beans
- twist ties

For each gift cone, use the pattern on page 155 and cut a cone from cream cardstock. Punch holes as indicated on the pattern. Stamp messages on one side of the cone. Trim the top edge with the craft scissors. Aligning the holes and spot gluing the tab to the inside of the opposite edge, fold the cone as indicated by the dashed lines on the pattern. Starting at the bottom of the cone and working in a crisscross pattern similar to lacing a tennis shoe, lace a 42" ribbon length through the holes and tie the ends into a bow at the top.

For the tag, layer and glue a ⁷/₈"x2⁵/₈" cream cardstock piece on a 1"x2³/₄" brown cardstock piece. Stamp "chocolate-covered espresso beans" on the tag. Punch 2 holes, ¹/₂" apart, near one end and thread the tag onto the center of a 13¹/₂" ribbon length. Fill a bag with Chocolate-Covered Espresso Beans and close with a twist tie. Tie the tag onto the bag and place the bag in the cone.

Chocolate-Covered Espresso Beans

Marshmallow Pops

FLOWER FROG JAR

- green striped scrapbook paper
- 18-gauge silver wire
- wire cutters
- alphabet beads and rub-ons
- silver crimp beads
- crimp and needle-nose pliers
- craft glue
- snowflake brad
- $1/16$" and $1/8$" dia. hole punches
- small silver jump rings
- silver clapperless bells
- green cardstock
- deckle-edged craft scissors
- green jumbo rickrack
- $5^3/4$"h x $2^1/2$" dia. green flower frog jar
- jute
- green fibers

For the jar tag, cut a $1^1/2$"x$2^3/8$" scrapbook paper piece and cut away the corners on one end. Spell "snowmen" on wire with alphabet beads and attach a crimp bead at each end. Bend the wire as desired and glue it to the tag. Attach the brad to the tag and use rub-ons to spell "are cool." Punch three $1/16$" holes, $1/2$" apart, along the bottom tag edge. Use jump rings to attach the bells through the holes. Glue the tag to cardstock. Using craft scissors on the bottom, cut the cardstock slightly larger than the tag. Punch a $1/8$" hole in the tag top. Knot rickrack around the jar. Tie the tag onto the rickrack with jute and fiber.

You can also dip pretzel rods in melted candy coating, then sprinkle with chopped nuts…arrange in a holiday glass filled with coarse sugar for a stand-up treat.

"Friendship is a precious gift to give at Christmas time. A cherished gift, a treasured gift that lasts through all time."

— *Unknown*

OH BOY! Marshmallow Pops

10-oz. bag marshmallows
16 wooden skewers (about 12 inches long)
14-oz. pkg. white candy coating, melted
orange and black decorating icing tubes

Place 2 marshmallows on each skewer; dip each into melted candy coating to coat marshmallows. Swirl off excess and place on wax paper to cool. Decorate with decorating icing. Wrap each in plastic wrap before giving. Makes 16.

~Denise Greenberg ★ Little Egg Harbor, NJ~

COOL & CREAMY
FUDGE BARS

*Everyone will enjoy receiving these
delicious bars!*

4 1-oz. squares unsweetened
    baking chocolate
$\frac{1}{2}$ c. plus 2 T. butter, divided
2 c. sugar
4 eggs, divided
1 t. vanilla extract
1 c. all-purpose flour
8-oz. pkg. cream cheese, softened
1 T. cornstarch
14-oz. can sweetened condensed milk
1 t. peppermint extract

Melt chocolate with $\frac{1}{2}$ cup butter in a
double boiler. Combine chocolate
mixture, sugar, 3 eggs, vanilla and flour
in a large mixing bowl; spread in a
greased 13"x9" baking pan. Bake at
350 degrees for 12 minutes. While
brownie layer is in oven, beat cream
cheese, remaining 2 tablespoons butter
and cornstarch until fluffy. Gradually
beat in milk, peppermint extract and
remaining egg; pour over brownie layer.
Bake at 350 degrees for 30 minutes
or until set. Top with glaze. Cool
completely, chill and cut into bars.
Makes 40.

Glaze:
1 c. semi-sweet chocolate chips
$\frac{1}{2}$ c. whipping cream

Combine all ingredients in a small
saucepan; melt over low heat, stirring
until thickened.

Cool & Creamy Fudge Bars

GINGHAM GIFT BOX

- green and brown kraft paper
- double-sided tape
- $\frac{1}{8}$" and $\frac{1}{4}$" dia. hole punches
- large-eye needle
- $\frac{1}{4}$"w and 1"w red ribbons
- alphabet, "Merry Christmas"
  and poinsettia stamps
- brown ink pad
- 8"wx9"hx4$\frac{3}{4}$"d gingham
  gift box

Cut a 4"x27" green paper piece and
tear a 3$\frac{1}{2}$"x27" brown paper piece.
Crumple, then flatten the brown
paper and tape it along the center
of the green. Starting and stopping
1$\frac{1}{2}$" from each end, punch a $\frac{1}{8}$" hole
every 1" (25 holes total) along each
long edge of the brown paper.

Use the needle to thread a 27"
length of $\frac{1}{4}$"w ribbon through the
holes along each long edge. Trim
and tape the ends to the back.
Stamp the paper as desired.
Overlapping and taping the ends
at the back, wrap the paper
around the box.

For the tag, cut a 1$\frac{3}{4}$"x3$\frac{1}{4}$" green
paper piece; round one end. Tear a
brown paper piece to fit on the tag.
Crumple, then flatten the paper
and tape it to the tag. Stamp
"FUDGE BARS" on the tag and
punch a $\frac{1}{4}$" hole at the top. Knot
the tag onto the center of a 22"
length of $\frac{1}{4}$"w ribbon. Tie the ends
along with a 17" length of 1"w ribbon
into a bow around the box handle.

BUCKET OF COOKIE MIX

This dough keeps for 3 months in the refrigerator, so make up the mix ahead of time to give for Christmas.

5 c. all-purpose flour
3³/₄ c. sugar
2 T. baking powder
2 t. salt
1¹/₂ c. plus 2 T. butter, softened

Combine first 4 ingredients in a very large mixing bowl; mix well. Cut in butter with a pastry blender until coarse crumbs form; place in an airtight container. Keeps in the refrigerator for up to 3 months. Attach instructions. Makes 10 cups.

Sunshine Cookies:

Bring 4 cups cookie mix to room temperature in a mixing bowl; add one egg, one tablespoon lemon zest and 1¹/₂ tablespoons lemon juice, mixing well. Divide dough in half; form each into a 1¹/₂-inch diameter roll. Wrap dough in plastic wrap; refrigerate until firm, about 2 hours. Cut into ¹/₈-inch slices; arrange one inch apart on greased baking sheets. Sprinkle with sugar; bake at 350 degrees for 8 minutes. Remove to a wire rack to cool completely. Makes about 4 dozen.

Brownies:

Bring 2 cups cookie mix to room temperature in a mixing bowl. Melt one cup semi-sweet chocolate chips; let cool 5 minutes and add to cookie mix. Stir 2 eggs and one teaspoon vanilla extract into mixture. Spread in a greased 8"x8" baking pan; bake at 350 degrees for 20 minutes. Set aside to cool. Melt one cup peanut butter chips; drizzle over the top. Cool. Cut into squares to serve. Makes 16.

RUDOLPH'S POPCORN BALLS

My mother made these every year when I was in elementary school. My sisters and I loved to help…my kids do the same thing in my kitchen today.

12 to 14 qts. popped popcorn
¹/₂ c. butter
16-oz. bag mini marshmallows
red food coloring

Place popcorn in a large roaster pan; set aside. Melt butter and marshmallows in a large saucepan over medium heat, stirring constantly. Remove from heat and stir in red food coloring to desired shade. Pour mixture over popcorn; stir well. Coat hands with butter and shape mixture into softball-size balls. Wrap each in plastic wrap. Makes 4 to 5 dozen.

Lacy Mayfield
Earth, TX

Brown bag it! Crinkle brown paper lunch bags and roll down the tops. Fill the bags with assorted nuts and snacks, place the bags in a basket and tuck in sprigs of greenery for a gift that's quick, pretty and tasty!

A well-spent day brings happy sleep.

—Leonardo DaVinci

Happiness lies in the joy of achievement and the thrill of creative effort.

— FRANKLIN DELANO ROOSEVELT

BUCKEYES

Here's a real treat for the peanut butter lovers on your list.

2 c. peanut butter
1/2 c. butter, softened
1 t. vanilla extract
1 lb. powdered sugar
3 c. semi-sweet chocolate chips

In a large mixing bowl, mix peanut butter, butter and vanilla together. Add powdered sugar, a small amount at a time, mixing by hand. Continue to add powdered sugar until mixture can be rolled into 1-inch balls that stay together. Melt chocolate in double boiler. Placing a ball on a fork, dip 3/4 of ball into chocolate. Place balls onto wax paper-lined baking sheet. Place in cool area or freezer to set. Makes 4 to 5 dozen.

Debbie Lloyd
Newark, OH

MINI MUFFIN TIN

Place Buckeyes in a mini muffin tin. Place the tin inside a cellophane bag and close with a twist tie. Knot ribbons around the top of the bag. For the tag, use circle punches to punch two 2³/₄" diameter circles from red cardstock and one 2¹/₈" diameter circle from green striped paper. With the green circle on top, layer and glue the circles together. Use rub-ons and a permanent pen to spell "holiday cheer" on the tag. Leaving the ends long, glue green chenille rickrack along the back edge of the tag; knot the ends around the bag.

*"May the spirit of giving
Go on through the year,
Bringing love, laughter,
Hope and good cheer."*

— Norma Woodbridge

Buckeyes

Initial Cookies

INITIAL COOKIES
Make a special initial cookie for all your friends!

$^3/_4$ c. butter, softened
1 c. powdered sugar
1 egg
$1^1/_2$ t. almond extract
$2^1/_2$ c. all-purpose flour
$^1/_8$ t. salt
4-inch high alphabet stencils

Beat butter and sugar in a large bowl until fluffy. Add egg and almond extract; beat until smooth. In a separate bowl, combine flour and salt. Add flour mixture to creamed mixture, stirring until a soft dough forms. Divide dough in half, wrap in plastic wrap and chill one hour. On a lightly floured surface, roll dough to $^1/_4$-inch thickness. Cut out initial cookies using stencils for the patterns; place on greased baking sheets. Bake at 350 degrees for 8 to 10 minutes; place cookies on a wire rack to cool. Ice cookies. Makes 2 dozen.

Icing:
3 c. powdered sugar
3 to 4 T. water
2 t. corn syrup
1 t. almond extract
red food coloring

Combine all ingredients except food coloring; stir until smooth. Tint $^1/_2$ cup icing red and spoon into a pastry bag fitted with a small round tip. Spoon remaining icing into another pastry bag fitted with a small round tip. Pipe white icing on cookies and allow to harden 30 minutes or place in refrigerator to harden faster. Pipe red icing on cookies and allow to harden.

Make it personal by giving your friends an Initial Cookie. For an added treat, give them a trio of cookies to represent their monogram!

COOKIE PACKAGE
For the background, cut a piece of illustration board or medium-weight cardboard to fit in a 4"x7$^7/_8$" cellophane bag. Cut two red cardstock pieces the same size and glue them to the background front and back.

For the bag topper, cut a 3$^1/_4$"x4" scrapbook paper piece. Trim $^1/_4$" from one long edge with scallop-edged craft scissors for the front. Fold the paper piece so the front long edge extends $^1/_2$" past the back long edge. Glue ribbon and wired pom-pom trim along the front edge. Place the background and an Initial Cookie in the cellophane bag. Fold the top of the bag to the back and sandwich it in the fold of the topper. Staple the topper to the bag.

For the tag, cut a 1"x2$^1/_8$" red cardstock piece and round one end. Glue the tag to brown scrapbook paper and cut the paper slightly larger than the tag. Punch a hole in the top of the tag. Layer and glue a torn scrapbook paper piece and a torn and stamped white cardstock piece on the tag. Knot ribbons through the hole in the tag. Use brads to attach silver snowflake charms to the tag. Use adhesive foam dots to attach the tag to the topper.

Seasoned greetings

Christmas is a time of celebrating...and cooking! When loved ones gather for the holidays, the merriment usually takes place around the dinner table. Kate, Holly & Mary Elizabeth know that a good meal stimulates good conversation, so they've served up an array of flavorful fare that's sure to get the party started! Their recipes will help you create festive feasts...from breakfast to dinner...not to mention all the delightful desserts and savory snacks in between!

Featuring Fruited Pork Loin, Dressed-up Holiday Stuffing and Parsley Biscuits, this mouthwatering meal is sure to satisfy! Each dish is a treat for the eyes, as well as the taste buds.

A Special Invitation Dinner

Host a holiday gathering the fun & easy way! For a Special Invitation Dinner, you prepare the main dish while giving each guest a different menu item to cook. Put a recipe in each invitation, and include a note that a similar dish may be substituted.

"Must-Have-Recipe" Salad

"MUST-HAVE-RECIPE" SALAD

A light, fruity salad that looks so pretty on a festive plate.

2 5-oz. pkgs. romaine lettuce
1 c. shredded Swiss cheese
1 c. cashews
1 apple, coarsely chopped
1 pear, coarsely chopped
¼ c. sweetened, dried cranberries

Combine all ingredients in a large serving bowl; toss to mix. Pour salad dressing over salad and toss. Serves 8 to 10.

Salad Dressing:
½ c. sugar
⅓ c. lemon juice
2 t. red onion, finely chopped
1 t. salt
⅔ c. oil
1 T. poppy seed

Combine sugar, lemon juice, onion and salt in blender container; cover and blend well. While blender is running, add oil in a slow, steady stream; blend until thick and smooth. Add poppy seed and blend an additional 10 seconds to mix.

Holly Peters
Lino Lakes, MN

FRUITED PORK LOIN

Slices of this pork loin make a beautiful holiday presentation.

½ c. dried dates, coarsely chopped
¼ c. dried apricots, coarsely chopped
¼ c. pecans, finely chopped
1 clove garlic, minced
1½ t. dried thyme, crushed
2 T. molasses, divided
½ t. salt, divided
¼ t. pepper
2-lb. boneless pork loin roast
⅔ c. bourbon or chicken broth
⅔ c. chicken broth
¼ c. whipping cream

Blend together dates, apricots, pecans, garlic, thyme, one tablespoon molasses, ¼ teaspoon salt and pepper; set aside. Butterfly pork loin roast by making a lengthwise cut down center of one side, cutting within ½ inch of the bottom. (Do not cut through roast.) Open roast, forming a rectangle. Starting at the center of the open loin, make another lengthwise cut on the left portion, cutting to within ½ inch of the edge. Repeat with right portion of the open loin. Spread date mixture evenly over open roast and starting with the short end, roll up stuffed roast jelly-roll style. Tie roast securely every 2 to 3 inches with kitchen string and place roast, seam side down, in a shallow roasting pan; set aside. Blend together bourbon or chicken broth, ⅔ cup chicken broth and remaining one tablespoon molasses in a small saucepan. Bring mixture to a boil and pour over roast. Roast pork at 350 degrees for one hour or until meat thermometer inserted into thickest portion registers 150 degrees, basting occasionally. Remove roast from roasting pan; reserve drippings. Cover roast with foil and let stand 10 minutes or until thermometer registers 160 degrees before slicing. Stir together cream and remaining ¼ teaspoon salt in a small saucepan; blend in reserved drippings. Cook over medium heat, stirring constantly, until mixture slightly thickens. Serve sauce with roast. Serves 6.

Tina Wright
Atlanta, GA

DRESSED-UP HOLIDAY STUFFING

My mother gave me this basic recipe 25 years ago and, over the years, I've added my own touches...either way, it's simply delicious!

2 24-oz. loaves, white bread
2 6.2-oz. pkgs. long-grain and
    wild rice, prepared
20 to 25 green onions, chopped
3 to 4 c. celery, chopped
2 c. slivered almonds
3 eggs, beaten
salt and pepper to taste
1 t. garlic, minced
dill weed to taste
1½ c. butter, melted

Tear bread into bite-size pieces; place in a very large bowl. Add rice, green onions, celery, almonds and eggs; mix well. Stir in salt, pepper, garlic and dill weed. Pour butter over stuffing; mix well. Place in two lightly greased 13"x9" glass baking dishes; bake, uncovered, at 350 degrees for one hour. Serves 16 to 20.

John Boyd Brandon
Jemez Springs, NM

PARSLEY BISCUITS

Enjoy these warm from the oven.

2 c. all-purpose flour
1 T. baking powder
½ t. salt
3 T. fresh parsley, chopped
zest of one lemon
½ c. vegetable shortening
½ c. milk
¼ c. whipping cream

In a large mixing bowl, combine flour, baking powder and salt; add parsley and lemon zest. Using a pastry cutter or 2 knives, cut in shortening until mixture resembles oatmeal. Add milk and cream; blend until mixture forms a ball. Place dough on a lightly floured surface and knead 5 times. Roll out dough to ½-inch thickness and cut out biscuits. Place on lightly greased baking sheets and bake at 425 degrees for 15 minutes or until golden. Makes eight 2½-inch biscuits.

Jo Ann

cream of Pumpkin SOUP

Make your own crusty loaf o' bread and serve a big Caesar salad with this soup...tasty!

★

2 T. butter
1 onion, diced
3 14-oz. cans chicken broth
29-oz. can pumpkin
2 carrots, chopped
1 T. brown sugar, packed
1 bay leaf
1 c. whipping cream
½ t. nutmeg
Garnish: fried ham cubes,
    optional

★

In a large saucepan, melt butter and sauté onion. Add broth, pumpkin, carrots, brown sugar & bay leaf. Bring to a boil, reduce heat and simmer for 15 minutes. Remove bay leaf. Purée mixture in blender and return to pan; stir in cream & nutmeg. Garnish with ham, if desired. Makes 8 servings.

~Janice Gilmer ★ Merrimack, NH~

Cream of Pumpkin Soup

91

SNOWFLAKE BREAD

Golden honey-glazed loaves with a snowflake design...so pretty for Christmas dinner.

1 pkg. active dry yeast
1/4 c. warm water
3/4 c. milk
1/2 c. butter, melted
1/4 c. honey
4 3/4 c. all-purpose flour, divided
2 eggs
2 t. vanilla extract
1 1/2 t. anise seed, crushed
1/2 t. salt

Combine yeast and warm water in a measuring cup; let stand 5 minutes. Combine milk, butter and honey in a large bowl. Stir in yeast mixture, 2 cups flour, eggs, vanilla, anise seed and salt. Beat with an electric mixer until smooth. Stir in another 2 cups flour until a soft dough forms. Turn dough onto a lightly floured surface; knead until smooth, gradually adding remaining 3/4 cup flour. Place in a greased bowl, turning dough to coat; cover and let rise 45 minutes or until double in bulk. Punch dough down and divide in half. Form each half into a 7 1/2-inch round loaf; place on greased baking sheets. Cover dough and let rise 15 minutes or until almost double in bulk. Use a knife to make a snowflake design in each loaf. Bake loaves at 350 degrees for 20 minutes. Brush glaze over loaves; return to oven for 5 to 10 minutes or until tops are golden. Serves 10 to 12.

Glaze:
1 egg, beaten
1 T. honey
1 T. water

Stir together all ingredients.

Vickie

Pickled Mushrooms

"We could always count on Grandma Spain to bring her pickled mushrooms to any family get-together... and they never lasted long! Even though she is no longer with us, we still think of her whenever someone makes this recipe."
— LINDA SPAIN ★ ASHLEY, OH —

1 onion, thinly sliced & separated into rings
1/3 c. red wine vinegar
1/3 c. oil
1 T. brown sugar, packed
2 t. dried parsley flakes
1 t. salt
1 t. yellow mustard
3 7-oz. jars button mushrooms, drained

In a small saucepan, combine all ingredients except mushrooms. When mixture comes to a boil, add mushrooms and simmer for 5 minutes. Pour into a bowl, cover & chill for several hours or overnight, stirring occasionally. Drain before serving. Makes 3 cups.

Snowflake Bread

HOT PECAN DIP

Very simple, yet elegant appetizer when served with baguette slices.

8-oz. pkg. cream cheese, softened
1 onion, grated
3-oz. pkg. dried beef, chopped
1/2 c. sour cream
1/4 c. green pepper, chopped
2 t. milk
1/4 t. pepper

Combine all ingredients; mix well. Spread in a buttered 9" pie pan; sprinkle with toasted pecans. Bake at 350 degrees for 20 minutes. Serves 12.

Toasted Pecans:
1/2 c. chopped pecans
2 t. butter, melted
1/4 t. salt

Toss all ingredients together; spread on an ungreased baking sheet. Broil until golden; stir often.

Jana Warnell
Kalispell, MT

CINNAMON & GINGER TREATS

You won't be able to stop nibbling on these.

3 c. assorted nuts
1 egg white
1 T. orange juice
2/3 c. sugar
1 t. cinnamon
1/2 t. ground ginger
1/2 t. allspice
1/4 t. salt

Place nuts in a large mixing bowl; set aside. Blend egg white and orange juice together until frothy; mix in remaining ingredients. Pour over nuts; mix thoroughly. Spread coated nuts onto an aluminum foil-lined baking sheet; bake at 275 degrees for 45 minutes, stirring every 15 minutes. Cool; store in an airtight container. Makes 3 cups.

Debbie Isaacson
Irvine, CA

Yam Risotto

YAM RISOTTO

Not your ordinary side dish.

2 T. butter
1 shallot, minced
1 clove garlic, minced
3/4 c. Arborio rice, uncooked
15.5-oz. can yams, mashed
3 c. chicken broth, divided
1/4 t. cinnamon
1/4 t. salt
1/8 t. pepper
3 T. pumpkin seeds, toasted
Garnish: toasted pumpkin seeds (optional)

Melt butter in a saucepan; add shallot and garlic. Sauté for one minute or until soft; stir in rice. Heat for one minute; mix in yams and 1/2 cup chicken broth. Heat until liquid is absorbed; stir in an additional 1/2 cup broth. Continue heating for 15 minutes, stirring constantly; add broth, 1/2 cup at a time, as previous additions have been absorbed. Remove from heat; stir in cinnamon, salt, pepper and 3 tablespoons pumpkin seeds. Sprinkle with additional pumpkin seeds, if desired. Serve warm. Serves 4.

Stephanie Moon
Nampa, ID

VEGETABLE BAKE

My Italian son-in-law first made this dish for our family on Thanksgiving...we love it!

13 1/4-oz. can mushroom pieces, drained
1 onion, diced
1/4 c. butter
10 3/4-oz. can cream of mushroom soup
10 3/4-oz. can cream of chicken soup
11-oz. can cut green beans, drained
11-oz. can yellow wax beans, drained
11-oz. can sliced carrots, drained
8-oz. pkg. shredded Cheddar cheese
8-oz. pkg. shredded mozzarella cheese

Sauté mushrooms and onion in butter until tender; add soups, beans and carrots. Remove from heat; spread into a 13" x 9" baking pan. Combine cheeses; sprinkle on top. Bake at 350 degrees about 30 minutes or until bubbly. Makes 12 to 15 servings.

Glory Bock
Lee's Summit, MO

Christmas Champagne Punch

CHRISTMAS CHAMPAGNE PUNCH

A good punch to start any occasion!

1 qt. frozen, unsweetened
    strawberries, thawed
1/2 to 1 c. sugar, to taste
2 bottles white Rhine or Moselle
    wine, chilled
1 bottle dry champagne, chilled
Garnish: fresh strawberries on
    wooden skewers (optional)

Crush fruit in a large bowl and stir
in sugar; allow sugar to dissolve.
Add wine and chill for 4 hours. Just
before serving, pour mixture into a
punch bowl and add champagne.
Garnish with fresh strawberries, if
desired. Makes 24 punch cups.

May our house always be too
small to hold all of our friends.
    —Traditional Holiday Toast

NEW ENGLAND PUMPKIN PIE

Make this special pie for your gathering.

6 T. brown sugar, packed
2 T. sugar
2 t. cinnamon
1/2 t. nutmeg
1/2 t. salt
1/4 t. ground cloves
1/2 c. molasses
3 eggs, separated
15-oz. can pumpkin
1 1/2 c. half-and-half
2 T. rum
2 9-inch pie crusts

Combine first 6 ingredients.
Add molasses and egg yolks; mix
well. Stir in pumpkin, half-and-half
and rum. Beat egg whites until
stiff; fold into pumpkin mixture.
Pour into unbaked pie crusts. Bake
at 425 degrees for 30 minutes or
until knife inserted in center comes
out clean. Serves 16.

Joan Merling
Bethel, CT

ORANGE SLICE CAKE

*This is my mom's gift to Dad every
Christmas and it's worth sharing
with others!*

1 c. butter, softened
2 c. sugar
5 eggs
1 T. vanilla extract
4 c. all-purpose flour, divided
1 t. salt
1/2 t. baking soda
3/4 c. buttermilk
2 c. pecans, chopped
8-oz. pkg. dates, chopped
1 lb. orange slice candies, chopped
4-oz. can flaked coconut

Beat together butter and sugar.
Add eggs, one at a time, beating
well after each addition; stir in
vanilla. In a separate bowl, combine
3 1/4 cups flour, salt and baking
soda; add to creamed mixture
alternating with buttermilk. In a
separate bowl, toss remaining
ingredients with remaining 3/4 cup
flour; fold into batter. Pour mixture
into a greased and floured 10" tube
pan. Bake at 300 degrees for
2 1/2 hours. Cool in pan 10 minutes;
invert onto platter and pour syrup
over top. Serves 10 to 12.

Syrup:
1/4 c. orange juice
1/4 c. lemon juice
1/2 c. powdered sugar

Combine all ingredients in a
saucepan and bring to a boil,
stirring until smooth.

Jennifer Allen
Tunas, MO

SWEET ALMOND COFFEE

Enjoy this sweet cocoa-almond blend on a frosty night.

1/2 c. sugar
1/4 c. baking cocoa
1/4 c. instant coffee granules
1/4 c. finely ground almonds
2 t. powdered non-dairy creamer
1/4 t. salt
4 1/2 c. milk

In an electric blender, combine sugar, cocoa, instant coffee, almonds, creamer and salt. Cover and blend on high speed for 10 seconds. Heat milk in a 2-quart saucepan. Do not boil. Add cocoa mixture to hot milk; stir to combine. Pour into mugs. Makes 5 cups.

Vickie

Sweet Almond Coffee &
Luscious Layered Brownies

Luscious Layered Brownies

No need to frost 'em... these are good just the way they are!

3/4 c. all-purpose flour
3/4 c. baking cocoa
1/4 t. salt
1/2 c. butter, sliced
1/2 c. sugar
1/2 c. brown sugar, packed
3 eggs, divided
2 t. vanilla extract
1 c. chopped pecans
3/4 c. white chocolate chips
1/2 c. caramel ice cream topping
3/4 c. semi-sweet chocolate chips

Mix together flour, cocoa & salt in a bowl; set aside. In another bowl, blend together butter & sugars until creamy. Add 2 eggs, one at a time, beating well after each addition. Mix in vanilla. Gradually beat in flour mixture. Reserve 3/4 cup batter; spread remaining batter into a greased 8"x8" baking pan. Sprinkle pecans & white chocolate chips over batter. Drizzle caramel topping over top. Beat remaining egg into reserved batter until light in color; stir in chocolate chips. Spread evenly over caramel topping. Bake at 350 degrees for 30 to 35 minutes. Cool & cut into squares. Makes 12 to 16.

All these recipes are so delicious, there may not be any food left over...but if there is, use take-out containers to send everyone home with a goodie box. You can also make a full set of recipe cards for each guest, so they can recreate the meal for themselves at a later time.

Orange Slice Cake

Stack ★ It ★ Up Breakfast

Flapjacks, griddlecakes, hotcakes…no matter what name you prefer for the traditional breakfast skillet bread, you're sure to call these new variations "scrumptious!" Be sure to try each one of these pancake and topping recipes. We think you'll find several new ways to start your holiday morning.

HAM & APPLE FILLED PUFFED PANCAKE

A hearty way to start your day!

3 T. butter, divided
3/4 c. milk
2/3 c. all-purpose flour
2 eggs
1/2 t. salt
1 c. cooked ham, cubed
21-oz. can apple pie filling
1 c. shredded Cheddar cheese

In a 9" glass pie plate, melt 2 tablespoons butter in oven. In a large bowl, combine milk, flour, eggs and salt. Using a wire whisk, beat until smooth; pour batter into pie plate. Bake, uncovered, at 400 degrees for 20 to 25 minutes or until golden brown. Meanwhile, in a 10" skillet, melt remaining one tablespoon butter until sizzling; add ham and apple pie filling. Cook over medium heat, stirring occasionally, until heated through. Spoon filling into center of hot pancake; sprinkle with cheese. Cut into wedges. Makes 4 servings.

Gail Prather
Bethel, MN

Ham & Apple Filled Puffed Pancake

Country Crunch Pancakes with Cinnamon, Pecan & Honey Syrup

COUNTRY CRUNCH PANCAKES

A favorite recipe that was shared with me by an Amish friend in our community. The crunchy topping makes these terrific!

2 c. all-purpose flour
$1/3$ c. whole-wheat flour
$1/2$ c. plus $1/3$ c. quick-cooking oats, divided
2 T. sugar
2 t. baking powder
1 t. baking soda
1 t. salt
2 t. cinnamon, divided
$2^1/4$ c. buttermilk
2 eggs, beaten
2 T. oil
1 c. blueberries
$1/4$ c. chopped almonds
$1/4$ c. brown sugar, packed

For batter, combine flours, $1/3$ cup oats, sugar, baking powder, baking soda, salt and one teaspoon cinnamon in a mixing bowl. In a separate bowl, combine buttermilk, eggs and oil. Stir into dry ingredients until blended. Fold in blueberries. For topping, mix together remaining $1/2$ cup oats and one teaspoon cinnamon. Blend in almonds and brown sugar. Sprinkle about one teaspoon topping for each pancake onto a hot, lightly greased griddle. Pour $1/4$ cup batter over topping. Immediately sprinkle with another teaspoonful of topping. Turn when bubbles form on top of pancakes. Cook until second side is golden brown. Makes 19.

Kathy Grashoff
Fort Wayne, IN

CINNAMON, PECAN & HONEY SYRUP

In our family, my husband always makes the pancakes and waffles!

2 c. maple syrup
$3/4$ c. chopped pecans
$1/2$ c. honey
$1/2$ t. cinnamon

Combine all ingredients; stir well. Pour mixture into an airtight container. Store at room temperature. Serve over waffles or pancakes. Makes 3 cups.

Flo Burtnett
Gage, OK

Lay pancakes on a baking sheet and place in a low oven to keep warm until all the batter is used.

BUTTERY MAPLE SYRUP

Leave out the butter for a more traditional maple syrup.

2 c. water
2 c. corn syrup
1 c. sugar
3 T. butter
$1/2$ t. salt
$1^1/2$ t. maple flavoring

Combine water, corn syrup, sugar, butter and salt in a heavy saucepan. Cook over medium heat until mixture reaches a full boil, stirring occasionally. Continue to boil syrup for 7 minutes; remove from heat and allow to cool for 15 minutes. Stir in maple flavoring; allow to cool to warm before serving. Makes one quart.

Regina Vining
Warwick, RI

Santa's favorite!

Jelly roll Pancakes

1 c. all-purpose flour
1½ t. baking powder
½ t. salt
1 c. milk
2 eggs
3 T. oil
⅓ c. jam or jelly
Garnish: Powdered Sugar

♥

Stir together flour, baking powder & salt in medium bowl; set aside. Blend together milk, eggs & oil in small bowl; stir into flour mixture 'til just blended. Drop by ½ cupfuls onto a hot, greased griddle. Cook pancakes on each side 'til lightly golden. Spread about 2 teaspoons jam or jelly on one side of each pancake; roll up, place seam-side down on serving plate and sprinkle with powdered sugar. Makes about eight 6-inch pancakes.

↪ A recipe from Renae Scheiderer
Beallsville, OH

♥ Idea!
Try Pumpkin Butter or Apple Butter instead of Jelly! Yum!

Buttermilk Pancakes with Orange Butter

ORANGE BUTTER

Spread on bagels, toast, muffins or pancakes...yummy!

1 c. butter, softened
2 t. orange zest
⅛ t. mace or nutmeg

Blend ingredients together until creamy; pack in a crock. Chill until ready to serve. Makes one cup.

Liz Plotnick-Snay
Gooseberry Patch

A *glassful of fresh-squeezed orange juice is always a treat at breakfast. Set out a juicer along with a bowl of oranges cut in half so everyone can take a turn at squeezing their own!*

BUTTERMILK PANCAKES

These pancakes are good and so easy to make...have the kids help!

1 c. all-purpose flour
3 T. sugar
1 t. baking powder
½ t. baking soda
½ t. salt
1 c. buttermilk
1 egg
2 T. butter, melted

In a large mixing bowl, combine flour, sugar, baking powder, baking soda and salt. Stir in remaining ingredients. Drop by ¼ cupfuls onto a hot, lightly greased griddle. Cook until bubbling; flip and cook other side. Use your favorite cookie cutter to cut out pancakes. Makes 4.

Jackie Crough
Salina, KS

Santa Face Pancakes

In the late 1940's, my father made these for breakfast on Christmas morn'. Served with whipped cream, we always had great fun making Santa's beard!

a recipe from Susan Young ♥ Madison, AL

1¼ c. all-purpose flour
2 T. sugar
3 t. baking powder
½ t. salt
1 egg

2 T. oil
3/4 to 1 c. milk
6 bacon slices, cut into fourths & cooked
Garnish: strawberry preserves & whipped cream

Sift dry ingredients into a large bowl. Make a well in the center and add egg, oil and 3/4 cup milk. Quickly stir until just blended; batter should not be thin. Add more milk if needed. When griddle is hot, pour ¼ cup batter per pancake onto griddle. When edges bubble, turn pancake over. Continue cooking until golden brown. Place pieces of bacon to resemble eyes, nose and mouth. Serve with preserves for Santa's hat and whipped cream for his beard and pom-pom. Makes 6 to 9 pancakes.

That is the BEST ~ to laugh with someone because you both think the same things are funny. - GLORIA VANDERBILT

CHOCOLATE CHIP PANCAKES

These ooey-gooey pancakes don't need syrup, but you'll want to make sure there are plenty of napkins on hand!

1 c. milk
2 eggs, beaten
2 c. buttermilk biscuit baking mix
¼ t. cinnamon
½ c. mini semi-sweet chocolate chips
Optional: powdered sugar

Combine first 4 ingredients, stirring until moistened. Fold in chocolate chips, being sure not to over blend. Drop by ¼ cupfuls onto a hot, greased griddle; flip over when bubbles appear around edges. Cook on each side until lightly golden. Sprinkle with powdered sugar, if desired. Makes 12 to 16.

Carolyn Demel
Houston, TX

DUBLIN POTATO PANCAKE

Yummy with eggs and bacon…a hearty farmhouse breakfast!

2 potatoes, shredded
1 onion, finely chopped
½ c. shredded Cheddar cheese
1 egg, beaten
2 bacon slices, cooked and chopped
salt and pepper to taste

Mix all ingredients together in a bowl. Spray a skillet with non-stick vegetable spray and place over medium-high heat until warm. Pour potato mixture into skillet, pressing down to form a pancake. Cook over medium-high heat until golden brown on the bottom and middle is set. Check edges periodically by gently lifting. Turn pancake using 2 spatulas and cook second side until golden. Serves 4.

Virginia Konerman
Virginia Beach, VA

Festive Tree-Trimming Feast

Trimming the Christmas tree is a popular holiday custom. And a tree-trimming party is just the thing to bring the family together for food and fun! The following pages are packed with delicious recipes…from a hearty Whole Baked Ham to Mom's Special Occasion Cherry Cake. Keep the festivities going with a tasty assortment of appetizers, drinks and desserts.

Whole Baked Ham & Sweet Hot Mustard

WHOLE BAKED HAM

A yummy ham that can be served hot or refrigerated and sliced for sandwiches.

12 to 14-lb. fully cooked boneless
    or bone-in ham
12 whole cloves
1½ c. pineapple juice
½ c. maple-flavored syrup
6 slices canned pineapple
1 c. water
¾ c. brown sugar, packed
3 T. mustard

Place ham, fat side up, in a shallow roasting pan. Press cloves into top of ham. Stir together pineapple juice and syrup; pour over ham. Arrange pineapple slices on ham. Bake at 325 degrees for 1½ hours. Add water and bake for 1½ additional hours. Remove from oven; remove pineapple slices. Mix together brown sugar and mustard; spread over ham. Bake an additional 30 minutes. Makes 18 to 20 servings.

Jacqueline Kurtz
Reading, PA

SWEET HOT MUSTARD

This mustard really spices up ham sandwiches.

2 2-oz. containers dry mustard
2¼ c. white vinegar
1½ c. sugar
¼ c. all-purpose flour
1 t. salt
¾ t. red pepper
1½ T. butter
3 eggs, lightly beaten

Combine mustard and vinegar in a large bowl; cover and let stand 8 hours. Combine sugar and next 3 ingredients; whisk into mustard mixture. Melt butter over medium heat. Add mustard mixture; cook 8 minutes or until slightly thickened. Gradually whisk about ¼ of hot mixture into beaten eggs; add to remaining hot mustard mixture, stirring constantly. Cook 3 minutes or until a thermometer registers 160 degrees and mixture is slightly thickened. Remove from heat. Cool completely. Store in an airtight container for up to 2 weeks. Makes 3 cups.

Brie Kisses

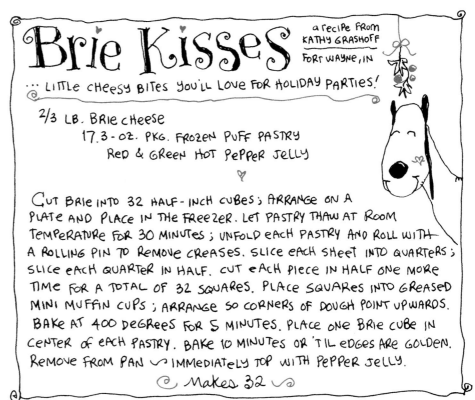

Brie Kisses

a recipe from
KATHY GRASHOFF
FORT WAYNE, IN

... LITTLE CHEESY BITES YOU'LL LOVE FOR HOLIDAY PARTIES!

2/3 LB. BRIE CHEESE
17.3-OZ. PKG. FROZEN PUFF PASTRY
RED & GREEN HOT PEPPER JELLY

CUT BRIE INTO 32 HALF-INCH CUBES; ARRANGE ON A PLATE AND PLACE IN THE FREEZER. LET PASTRY THAW AT ROOM TEMPERATURE FOR 30 MINUTES; UNFOLD EACH PASTRY AND ROLL WITH A ROLLING PIN TO REMOVE CREASES. SLICE EACH SHEET INTO QUARTERS; SLICE EACH QUARTER IN HALF. CUT EACH PIECE IN HALF ONE MORE TIME FOR A TOTAL OF 32 SQUARES. PLACE SQUARES INTO GREASED MINI MUFFIN CUPS; ARRANGE SO CORNERS OF DOUGH POINT UPWARDS. BAKE AT 400 DEGREES FOR 5 MINUTES. PLACE ONE BRIE CUBE IN CENTER OF EACH PASTRY. BAKE 10 MINUTES OR 'TIL EDGES ARE GOLDEN. REMOVE FROM PAN ⌣ IMMEDIATELY TOP WITH PEPPER JELLY.

Makes 32

BURGUNDY MEATBALLS

This recipe has become a New Year's favorite in our house!

1¹/₂ lbs. ground beef
¹/₃ c. milk
¹/₄ c. bread crumbs
1 egg, beaten
1¹/₂ t. salt
¹/₈ t. pepper
2 T. dried, minced onion, divided
1 T. butter
1¹/₂ T. all-purpose flour
¹/₄ t. garlic powder
1 c. beef broth
2 T. tomato paste
¹/₂ c. raisins
Optional: ¹/₄ c. burgundy wine or
    cranberry juice

Mix first 6 ingredients together; add one tablespoon onion. Shape into 18 balls; brown in butter in a skillet. Remove meatballs; whisk flour and garlic powder into drippings in skillet. Stir in remaining onion, beef broth, tomato paste and raisins; add meatballs. Cover and simmer for 10 minutes. Remove meatballs to a hot serving dish; stir wine or juice into remaining sauce in skillet, if desired. Heat and pour sauce over meatballs before serving. Serves 4 to 6.

Suzanne Flinn
Bedford, IN

WRAPPED WATER CHESTNUTS

Crunchy with just the right amount of sweetness.

1 lb. bacon, slices halved
16-oz. can whole water chestnuts
¹/₂ c. mayonnaise
¹/₂ c. brown sugar, packed
¹/₄ c. chili sauce

Cook bacon until almost crisp; drain. Wrap one slice around each water chestnut; secure with a toothpick. Arrange in an ungreased 9"x9" baking pan; set aside. Mix remaining ingredients together; pour over water chestnuts. Bake at 350 degrees for 45 minutes. Makes about 2 dozen.

Jan Fishback
Carmi, IL

PINEAPPLE BALL

Serve with an assortment of crackers and bread sticks and watch it disappear!

2 8-oz pkgs. cream cheese,
    softened
2 T. green pepper, chopped
2 T. onion, finely chopped
2 t. seasoned salt
¹/₄ c. crushed pineapple, drained
2 T. sugar
2 c. chopped pecans, divided

Mix first 6 ingredients with one cup pecans; shape into a ball. Cover and chill one hour. Roll in remaining one cup pecans; cover with plastic wrap and refrigerate until firm. Makes about 2¹/₂ cups.

Janice Patterson
Black Forest, CO

Pineapple Ball

Citrus Mimosa

HOMEMADE EGGNOG

There's nothing like the taste of homemade eggnog...sprinkle with cinnamon or nutmeg before serving.

²/₃ c. sugar
4 egg yolks
¹/₂ t. salt
4 c. milk
8 c. half-and-half
nutmeg to taste
1 pt. whipping cream, chilled
3 T. sugar
2 t. vanilla extract
Garnish: frozen whipped topping, thawed and cinnamon or nutmeg

Beat sugar into egg yolks in a saucepan; add salt and stir in milk. Cook mixture over medium heat, stirring constantly, until mixture coats the back of a metal spoon. Remove from heat and set pan in ice water to cool quickly. Pour through a sieve to remove lumps. Add half-and-half to cooled mixture; sprinkle with nutmeg. In a separate bowl, whip cream with sugar and vanilla; fold into egg mixture. Stir well before serving. Serve with a dollop of whipped topping and a sprinkle of cinnamon or nutmeg. Makes 12 servings.

Rebecca Ferguson
Carlisle, AR

Citrus Mimosa

makes the champagne go a little further!

∘∘ ☆ ∘∘

1 c. PREPARED STRAWBERRY DAIQUIRI MIX

6 OZ. COLD WATER

6-OZ. CAN FROZEN ORANGE JUICE CONCENTRATE, THAWED

3/4 c. FRESH GRAPEFRUIT JUICE

1/3 c. FROZEN LEMONADE CONCENTRATE, THAWED

3 T. FROZEN LIMEADE CONCENTRATE, THAWED

1 BOTTLE CHAMPAGNE*, CHILLED

garnish: orange rind curls

∘∘∘ ☆ ∘∘∘∘

COMBINE PREPARED DAIQUIRI MIX, WATER, ORANGE JUICE CONCENTRATE, GRAPEFRUIT JUICE, LEMONADE & LIMEADE CONCENTRATES IN A PITCHER OR BOWL. STIR 'TIL WELL COMBINED. COVER & CHILL. TO SERVE, POUR AN EQUAL AMOUNT OF THE CHILLED JUICE MIXTURE & CHAMPAGNE INTO 8 GLASSES. GARNISH WITH ORANGE RIND CURLS. MAKES 8 SIX-OUNCE SERVINGS.

* Note: For a non-alcoholic drink, substitute carbonated water for the champagne!

BLACK & WHITE SALSA

This salsa looks as great as it tastes.

15¹/₂-oz. can black beans, rinsed
    and drained
10-oz. pkg. shoe peg frozen corn,
    partially thawed
1 bunch green onions, diced
1 red tomato, diced
1 yellow tomato, diced
juice of 2 limes
1 jalapeño pepper, diced
1 T. olive oil
¹/₂ t. salt
¹/₈ t. pepper
fresh cilantro, chopped, to taste

Combine beans, corn, onions
and tomatoes; set aside. Mix
remaining ingredients together;
combine mixtures before serving.
Makes 3 to 4 cups.

Kristen Halverson
Folsom, CA

SWEET RED PEPPER DIP

*Serve this with fresh vegetables and
bagel chips.*

2 sweet red peppers
1 c. sour cream
2 3-oz. pkgs. cream cheese
¹/₄ t. salt
¹/₄ t. paprika
¹/₈ t. cayenne pepper

Cut sweet red peppers in half
lengthwise; remove stems and
seeds. Place peppers, cut side
down, in an 8"x8" baking dish.
Cover and microwave on high for
8 to 10 minutes or until peppers
are tender. Put peppers in cold
water and remove skins. Combine
peppers and remaining ingredients
in a food processor or blender and
process until smooth. Refrigerate
12 hours before serving. Makes about
1³/₄ cups.

Liz Plotnick-Snay
Gooseberry Patch

CRAB-STUFFED MUSHROOMS

*A delicious appetizer...plan to
make extras!*

6-oz. can crabmeat
³/₄ c. grated Parmesan cheese
¹/₂ c. butter, melted
¹/₃ c. bread crumbs
2 to 3 cloves garlic, chopped
¹/₄ to ¹/₂ c. onion, chopped
salt and pepper to taste
12-oz. pkg. fresh mushrooms, caps
    washed and stems removed

Mix all ingredients together, except
mushrooms. Stuff mushroom caps
with crab mixture and place on a
lightly oiled baking sheet. Bake at
375 degrees for 20 minutes.
Makes about 15.

Nicole Shira
New Baltimore, MI

A RECIPE FROM
BRENDA HARRELL ★ BEULAVILLE, NC

CARAMEL APPLE DIP

QUICK & EASY - PERFECT TO BRING TO
A WINTER GATHERING!

★

8-OZ. PKG. CREAM CHEESE, SOFTENED
½ C. CARAMEL ICE CREAM TOPPING
¼ C. HONEY
¼ T. CINNAMON
3 TO 4 GREEN & RED APPLES,
    CORED & SLICED

GARNISH: Cinnamon

★

IN A MEDIUM SERVING BOWL,
COMBINE CREAM CHEESE, CARAMEL
TOPPING, HONEY & ¼ TEASPOON
CINNAMON; BEAT UNTIL SMOOTH.
STORE IN REFRIGERATOR 'TIL
CHILLED. SPRINKLE WITH CINNAMON
AND SERVE WITH APPLE SLICES.
~ Makes 2 cups ~

Caramel Apple Dip

Raspberry Bars & Coffee Hermits

MOM'S SPECIAL OCCASION CHERRY CAKE

A special occasion cake.

2^1/$_4$ c. cake flour
2^1/$_2$ t. baking powder
^{1}/$_4$ t. salt
^{1}/$_2$ c. shortening
1^1/$_3$ c. sugar
3 egg whites
^{2}/$_3$ c. milk
10-oz. jar maraschino cherries,
    drained with juice reserved
^{1}/$_2$ c. chopped walnuts
4-oz. jar maraschino cherries
    with stems

Combine flour, baking powder and salt in a small bowl; set aside. Beat shortening in a large bowl for 30 seconds; beat in sugar. Gradually add egg whites, beating well after each addition; set aside. Whisk milk and ^{1}/$_4$ cup reserved cherry juice together; add alternately with flour mixture to sugar mixture, mixing well. Fold in nuts and drained cherries; divide batter evenly and pour into 2 lightly greased and floured 8" round baking pans. Bake at 350 degrees for 25 to 30 minutes; cool on a wire rack for 10 minutes. Remove from pans to cool completely; spread frosting between layers and on the top and sides of cake. Decorate top with a ring of stemmed cherries. Makes 8 to 10 servings.

Butter Frosting:
^{3}/$_4$ c. butter, softened
6 c. powdered sugar, divided
^{1}/$_3$ c. milk
^{1}/$_4$ t. salt
1^1/$_2$ t. vanilla extract
4 to 6 drops red food coloring

Beat butter until fluffy; mix in 3 cups powdered sugar. Gradually blend in milk, salt and vanilla; add remaining 3 cups powdered sugar, mixing well. Stir in food coloring to desired tint.

Roger Baker
La Rue, OH

RASPBERRY BARS

Whip up these fruity treats for a potluck and watch them disappear!

1 c. butter, softened
^{3}/$_4$ c. sugar
1 egg
^{1}/$_2$ t. vanilla extract
2^1/$_2$ c. all-purpose flour
10-oz. jar seedless raspberry jam
^{1}/$_2$ c. chopped pecans, toasted

Beat butter and sugar until creamy. Add egg and vanilla, beating until blended. Add flour, beating until blended. Reserving one cup dough, press remaining dough firmly into a lightly greased 9"x9" baking pan. Spread jam evenly over crust. Stir pecans into reserved one cup dough. Sprinkle evenly over jam layer. Bake at 350 degrees for 25 to 28 minutes or until golden. Cool completely on a wire rack. Makes about 1^1/$_2$ dozen.

*S*et the mood for your tree-trimming party by playing Christmas music. Whether you select traditional holiday hymns or whimsical songs, be sure to have the family sing along!

COFFEE HERMITS

A delicious coffee-flavored cookie.

^{1}/$_2$ c. shortening
1 c. brown sugar, packed
1 egg
2 T. water
1^1/$_2$ c. all-purpose flour
2 t. instant coffee granules
^{1}/$_2$ t. baking soda
^{1}/$_2$ t. cinnamon
^{1}/$_4$ t. salt
^{1}/$_4$ t. nutmeg
^{1}/$_2$ c. raisins
^{1}/$_2$ c. chopped pecans
^{1}/$_2$ c. chocolate chips

Combine shortening and brown sugar; blend in egg. Add water and set aside. Combine next 6 ingredients; mix into sugar mixture. Fold in remaining ingredients; drop rounded teaspoonfuls of dough about 2 inches apart onto lightly greased baking sheets. Bake at 350 degrees for 10 minutes. Makes about 5 dozen.

Pamela Raybon
Edna, TX

It All Starts With A Cake Mix

Whipping up a batch of delicious baked goods for your holiday entertaining and gift giving is a piece of cake! Just start with a package of cake mix and you can easily bake muffins, cookies, bars, brownies and of course, cakes.

...in all things, the supreme excellence is simplicity.
— LONGFELLOW —

Sugar-Topped Muffins

SUGAR-TOPPED MUFFINS

Enjoy these warm muffins for a real treat!

18¼-oz. pkg. white cake mix
1 c. milk
2 eggs
½ t. nutmeg
⅓ c. sugar
½ t. cinnamon
¼ c. butter, melted

Blend cake mix, milk, eggs and nutmeg on low speed with an electric mixer until just moistened; beat on high speed for 2 minutes. Fill paper-lined muffin cups ⅔ full. Bake at 350 degrees until golden, about 15 to 18 minutes. Cool for 5 minutes. Combine sugar and cinnamon on a small plate. Brush muffin tops with butter; roll in sugar and cinnamon mixture. Serve warm. Makes 2 dozen.

As a little girl, I can remember going to my grandparents' house to help bake Christmas cookies. Mother would tell my brother and me to come to Grandmother's house right after school that day. All day long while in school, I would be daydreaming about baking cookies. We would eat supper and then start baking the delicious butter cookies. Grandmother always gave my mother more than half of the fresh-baked cookies to take home, but when we would visit, she always had plenty of cookies for us there, too! I looked forward to this time every year.

— Henrietta Loveland
Baltimore, MD

Devil's Food Sandwich Cookies

Devil's Food Sandwich Cookies

...great for dunking!

a recipe from
Sheila Gwaltney
★ Johnson City, TN

18¼-oz. pkg. Devil's Food cake mix
¾ c. shortening
2 eggs
8-oz. pkg. cream cheese, softened
½ c. margarine, softened
½ t. almond extract
16-oz. pkg. powdered sugar

Combine cake mix, shortening & eggs. Form into small balls and flatten slightly on ungreased baking sheet. Bake at 350 degrees for 8 to 10 minutes. In medium bowl, blend cream cheese, margarine & almond extract. Gradually blend in powdered sugar until desired consistency. Beat with a spoon 'til smooth; refrigerate. When cookies are cool, spread filling between 2 cookies; repeat. Keep refrigerated. Makes 2 dozen.

PISTACHIO CAKE

A popular cake in the 1970's...it's still very good, easy to make and looks so festive!

18¹/₄-oz. pkg. white cake mix
3.4-oz. pkg. instant pistachio
    pudding mix
1 c. oil
1 c. club soda
3 eggs
¹/₂ c. pistachios, chopped
Garnish: chopped pistachios

Combine all ingredients; blend for 4 minutes. Pour batter into a greased and floured 10" tube pan; bake at 350 degrees for 45 to 50 minutes or until toothpick inserted in center of cake comes out clean. Cool in pan for 10 to 15 minutes; remove and cool completely on a wire rack. Frost and garnish with nuts; refrigerate until ready to serve. Makes 12 servings.

Frosting:
2 envelopes whipped topping mix
1¹/₂ c. cold milk
3.4-oz. pkg. instant pistachio
    pudding mix

Combine whipped topping mix and milk; beat until soft peaks form. Add pudding mix; beat until fluffy.

Ethel Bolton
Vienna, VA

KATE'S HOLIDAY DREAM: PEPPERMINT SWIRL ICE CREAM and A GIGANTIC CHOCOLATE CUPCAKE WITH SPRINKLES ON TOP!

Pistachio Cake

GRANDMA GRACIE'S LEMON CAKE

This recipe has become a New Year's favorite at our house!

18¹/₄-oz. pkg. yellow cake mix
3.4-oz. pkg. instant lemon pudding mix
³/₄ c. oil
³/₄ c. water
4 eggs

Mix together all ingredients. Pour into a greased 13"x9" baking pan. Bake at 350 degrees for 35 to 40 minutes or until toothpick inserted in center comes out clean. Remove cake from oven and immediately poke holes through the cake with a fork; pour glaze over top. Serves 10 to 12.

Glaze:
2 c. powdered sugar
¹/₃ c. lemon juice
2 T. butter, melted
2 T. water

Combine all ingredients.

Denise Grace Musgrave
Shelbyville, IN

RASPBERRY UPSIDE-DOWN CAKE

Great served warm or cold and it couldn't be easier to prepare!

18¹/₄-oz. pkg. yellow cake mix and
    ingredients to prepare cake
1 c. raspberries
³/₄ c. sugar
¹/₂ c. whipping cream

Prepare cake mix according to package directions. Pour into greased and floured 10" cake pan. Place raspberries over top of cake mix. Sprinkle sugar over raspberries. Gently pour whipping cream over top. Bake for 25 to 35 minutes in a 350 degree oven. Let stand for 10 minutes. Turn upside down on plate to serve. Makes 10 to 12 servings.

Becky Rogers
Saline, MI

Keep plenty of cake mix on hand so you can be ready to bring a sweet treat to any holiday get-together.

PUMPKIN CRISP

Everyone comes together at dinnertime when they know there's pumpkin crisp for dessert!

16-oz. can pumpkin
12-oz. can evaporated milk
3 eggs
1 c. sugar
2 t. cinnamon
18¼-oz. pkg. yellow cake mix
1½ c. chopped pecans
1 c. margarine, melted
8-oz. pkg. cream cheese, softened
½ c. powdered sugar
¾ c. thawed whipped topping

Mix pumpkin, milk, eggs, sugar and cinnamon together with mixer until well blended. Pour into greased 13"x9" baking pan. Sprinkle dry cake mix over the top. Sprinkle pecans over cake mix. Drizzle margarine over all; don't stir. Bake at 350 degrees for one hour. Cool and invert on a large platter. Blend together cream cheese, powdered sugar and whipped topping and spread over cooled crisp. Refrigerate until ready to serve. Makes 10 to 12 servings.

Judy Wilson
Hutchinson, MN

NUT ROLL BARS

Kids gobble up these rich and tasty treats.

18¼-oz. pkg. yellow cake mix
¼ c. butter, melted
1 egg
3 c. mini marshmallows
2 c. peanuts, chopped
2 c. crispy rice cereal
10-oz. pkg. peanut butter chips
½ c. corn syrup
½ c. butter
1 t. vanilla extract

Combine cake mix, butter and egg; press into a 13"x9" baking pan. Bake at 350 degrees for 10 to 12 minutes. Arrange marshmallows on top and return to oven for about 3 minutes or until marshmallows puff up. Combine peanuts and cereal. Melt peanut butter chips, corn syrup and butter in a saucepan over low heat; stir in vanilla. Pour mixture over peanuts and cereal mixture, stirring to coat; spread evenly over marshmallow layer. Refrigerate overnight and cut into bars. Makes 2 dozen.

Shelly Schenkel
Sioux Falls, SD

DROP THAT BACKPACK and DIG IN! MOM'S GOT

CARAMEL Brownies

... a great after-school treat with a glass of icy-cold cider!

✶

14-oz. pkg. caramels, unwrapped
2/3 c. evaporated milk, divided
18¼-oz. pkg. German chocolate cake mix
2/3 c. butter, melted
1 c. chopped pecans
12-oz. pkg. chocolate chips

✶

Combine caramels & 1/3 cup evaporated milk in a microwave-safe bowl. Heat, stirring occasionally, until caramels have melted; set aside. Combine cake mix, butter, remaining 1/3 cup evaporated milk & pecans. Press half of cake mixture into bottom of greased & floured 13"x9" baking pan. Bake at 350 degrees for 8 minutes; remove from oven. Sprinkle with chocolate chips; spread caramel mixture over the top. Drop remaining cake mixture by spoonfuls on top of caramel mixture; bake an additional 15 to 18 minutes. Cool slightly; refrigerate 30 minutes to firm caramel layer. Cut into bars. Makes 2 dozen.

~Jody Komarnitzki ✶ Venice, FL~

Nut Roll Bars

What can you do when you're far from family and can't go "home" for the holidays? Transform your traditions! Some of your friends probably can't have Christmas with their families either, so invite them over to enjoy a combination of customs. Have guests bring dishes that reflect their family's regional or ethnic heritage. We've included recipes for some universal favorites to help you get the party started.

Herb-Roasted Holiday Turkey

HERB-ROASTED HOLIDAY TURKEY

So easy...just pop the turkey in a roasting bag!

1 T. all-purpose flour
1 onion, sliced
2 stalks celery, chopped
1 carrot, chopped
12 to 16-lb. turkey
2 T. oil
1 T. dried sage
1 t. dried thyme
1 t. dried rosemary
1 t. seasoned salt
1 t. pepper

Shake flour in a turkey-size oven bag; arrange in a 2-inch deep roasting pan. Add vegetables to bag; set aside. Remove neck and giblets from turkey and reserve for another use; rinse turkey, pat dry and brush with oil. Combine herbs, salt and pepper; sprinkle over turkey. Place turkey in bag on top of vegetables; close bag with nylon tie provided and tuck ends into pan. Cut six 1/2-inch slits in top of bag; insert meat thermometer into thickest part of inner thigh. Bake at 350 degrees for 2 to 2 1/2 hours or until meat thermometer reads 180 degrees. Let stand in bag for 15 minutes before opening; pour off drippings and reserve for gravy. Serves 10 to 12.

Turkey Gravy:
drippings from roasted turkey
1/4 c. all-purpose flour
1/4 t. salt
1/4 t. poultry seasoning

Pour drippings into a large, deep bowl. Spoon off fat, reserving 3 to 4 tablespoons; discard remaining fat. Measure drippings; add water, if necessary, to equal 2 1/2 cups.

Place reserved fat in a skillet; stir in flour, salt and poultry seasoning. Heat over medium-high heat, stirring constantly until smooth and bubbly, about one minute. Gradually stir drippings into flour mixture; heat to boiling, stirring frequently. Boil for 5 to 7 minutes until thickened. Makes about 2 cups.

Vickie

GREAT-GRANDMA'S DRESSING

My Italian great-grandmother would make this dish for holidays and special occasions. It's almost a meal in itself!

2 T. olive oil
1 lb. mushrooms, sliced
5 stalks celery, chopped
1 onion, chopped
3 cloves garlic, minced
8-oz. stick pepperoni, chopped
4-oz. can sliced black olives
3/4 c. fresh parsley, chopped
1 t. poultry seasoning
pepper to taste
15 to 18 slices bread, torn
1 1/2 t. chicken bouillon granules

Heat oil in a large skillet; add mushrooms, celery, onion and garlic. Sauté for 5 minutes over medium heat. Add pepperoni, olives, parsley, poultry seasoning and pepper; sauté 5 additional minutes. Place bread in a lightly greased 13"x9" baking pan; mix in sautéed mixture until moistened. Gradually stir in chicken bouillon. Bake at 325 degrees for 40 to 45 minutes. Serves 4 to 6.

Lori Van Aken
Arvada, CO

Get the kids in on the fun by having them make traditional Christmas crafts from various countries around the world.

ALOHA CHICKEN WINGS

A staple at any gathering.

1/4 c. butter
1/2 c. catsup
1 clove garlic, minced
3 lbs. chicken wings
1 c. bread crumbs
14-oz. can pineapple chunks,
    drained and juice reserved
2 T. brown sugar, packed
1 T. whole ginger, minced
1 T. Worcestershire sauce
hot pepper sauce to taste

Place butter in a jelly-roll pan; heat in a 400-degree oven until melted. Stir catsup and garlic together; brush over wings. Coat with bread crumbs; arrange in jelly-roll pan, turning to coat both sides with melted butter. Bake at 400 degrees for 30 minutes. While baking, add enough water to reserved pineapple juice to equal 3/4 cup liquid; pour into a small mixing bowl. Whisk in remaining ingredients; pour over wings. Continue baking until juices run clear when chicken is pierced with a fork, about 20 to 30 additional minutes. Place pineapple around wings, baking until heated through. Serves 4.

Dianne Gregory
Sheridan, AR

DEBBIE'S LONG-DISTANCE MICHIGAN CORN CHIP DIP

This will serve a large group.

16 oz. cream cheese, softened
32 oz. sour cream
1 t. seasoned salt
1 tomato, chopped
6 green onions, sliced
6-oz. can large pitted olives,
    drained and sliced
8 oz. Colby or mild Cheddar
    cheese, shredded
Garnish: parsley, paprika and
    green onions

Beat cream cheese until fluffy. Add sour cream and mix thoroughly. Add seasoned salt. Add tomato, onion and olives. Mix sour cream mixture with tomato mixture. Pour into a 13"x9" dish. Sprinkle cheese on top of dip mixture. Garnish with parsley, paprika and green onions. Serve with corn chips, vegetables, dip-size chips or round butter-flavored crackers. Makes about 6 cups.

Dawn Marshall

POLENTA WITH TOMATO

Polenta is an Italian version of cornmeal mush...it's good, try it!

2 c. water
1/2 c. cornmeal
1/2 t. salt
1 c. onion, chopped
1 clove garlic, minced
1 T. oil
2 t. dried marjoram, divided
1 tomato, cut into 6 slices
1/4 c. crumbled Gorgonzola cheese

Bring water to a boil; stir in cornmeal and salt. Cook, stirring constantly, until mixture thickens and comes to a boil; boil one minute. Cover and cook over low heat 7 minutes. Remove from heat; cool to room temperature. Sauté onion and garlic in oil; add one teaspoon marjoram. Stir onion mixture into polenta; spread into a greased 11"x7" baking dish. Cover and refrigerate at least 6 hours. Cut into 6 squares and arrange on a lightly greased baking sheet. Bake at 425 degrees for 25 minutes; top each square with one tomato slice. Sprinkle with cheese and remaining one teaspoon marjoram; bake for 5 minutes or until cheese begins to melt. Serve warm. Makes 6 servings.

Gail Prather
Bethel, MN

"Friendship! mysterious cement of the soul!
Sweetener of life! and solder of society!"

— Robert Blair

Polenta with Tomato

CREOLE GREEN BEANS

A wonderful green bean side dish — a twist on the usual recipe!

6 bacon slices, crisply cooked,
    crumbled and drippings reserved
1/2 c. green pepper, chopped
1/4 c. onion, chopped
2 T. all-purpose flour
2 T. brown sugar, packed
1 T. Worcestershire sauce
1/2 t. salt
1/4 t. pepper
1/8 t. dry mustard
16-oz. can peeled whole tomatoes,
    cut into fourths
16-oz. can green beans, drained

In skillet with bacon drippings, sauté green pepper and onion until tender. Blend together next 6 ingredients; stir into skillet. Add tomatoes and continue to stir until mixture thickens. Add green beans and heat through; sprinkle with crumbled bacon. Serves 6.

Cheryl Chapman
Union, MO

TAKE-ALONG POTATOES

My family's favorite potato dish!

10 to 12 potatoes, peeled
    and thinly sliced
1 to 2 onions, sliced
2/3 c. shredded Cheddar cheese
1/2 c. butter, melted
15-oz. can chicken broth
1 T. dried parsley
2 T. Worcestershire sauce
salt and pepper to taste

In a greased 13"x9" pan, layer potatoes, onion and cheese. Pour butter over mixture. Mix remaining ingredients and pour over mixture. Bake, covered, at 425 degrees for 45 to 50 minutes or until potatoes are tender. Uncover, turn off oven and leave dish in oven for 10 minutes. Makes 10 to 12 servings.

Linda Murdock
Selah, WA

Creole Green Beans

Baked Butternut Squash and Apples

This is an old-fashioned recipe from the Midwest; the apples and maple syrup are wonderful together!

2 butternut squash, peeled & seeded
2 1/4 lbs. Granny Smith apples, peeled & cored
3/4 c. dried currants
freshly grated nutmeg
Salt & pepper to taste
3/4 c. maple syrup
1/4 c. butter, cut into pieces
1 1/2 T. fresh lemon juice

Cut squash & apples crosswise into 1/4 inch slices. Cook squash in large pot of boiling, salted water for 3 minutes or until almost tender. Drain well. Combine squash, apples & currants in 13" x 9" glass baking dish. Season with desired amounts of nutmeg, salt & pepper. Combine maple syrup, butter & lemon juice in small saucepan. Whisk over low heat 'til butter melts. Pour syrup over squash mixture and toss to coat evenly. Bake at 350 degrees until squash and apples are very tender, about one hour, stirring occasionally. Cool 5 minutes. Makes 8 servings.

OH BOY! Olliebollen (DOUGHNUTS)

A FAVORITE CHRISTMAS MORNING TRADITION FROM OUR DUTCH ANCESTORS, BUT GOOD ANY TIME, ANY DAY!

1 PKG. ACTIVE DRY YEAST
1 t. SUGAR
1/4 c. WARM WATER
2 1/4 c. CAKE FLOUR
1 1/2 c. RAISINS
1 c. WARM MILK (100 to 110 DEGREES)
1/4 c. SUGAR
1 EGG, BEATEN
3/4 t. CINNAMON
1/2 t. SALT
1/4 t. NUTMEG
OIL
1 c. POWDERED SUGAR

DISSOLVE YEAST WITH ONE TEASPOON SUGAR & WATER—LET SIT FOR ABOUT 10 MINUTES. IN LARGE BOWL, COMBINE THE NEXT 8 INGREDIENTS 'TIL WELL BLENDED; ADD YEAST MIXTURE. COVER & LET RISE FOR ONE HOUR. DROP 2 TABLESPOONFULS OF DOUGH INTO HOT OIL IN DEEP FRYER; FRY 'TIL GOLDEN BROWN. DRAIN ON PAPER TOWELS. ROLL IN POWDERED SUGAR. SERVE IMMEDIATELY. MICROWAVE TO REHEAT. MAKES 2 DOZEN.

~ SALLY BORLAND ★ PORT GIBSON, NY ~

Dakota Bread

DAKOTA BREAD

Mom always has this hearty bread waiting in the cupboard when we visit. It's named for all the good grains in it, which are grown in the Dakotas.

1 pkg. active dry yeast
1/2 c. warm water
1/2 c. cottage cheese
1/4 c. honey
1 egg
2 T. oil
1 t. salt
2 1/4 c. bread flour, divided
1/2 c. whole-wheat flour
1/4 c. wheat germ, toasted
1/4 c. rye flour
1/4 c. long-cooking oats, uncooked
2 T. cornmeal
1 egg white, beaten
2 T. sunflower kernels

Combine yeast and water in a small bowl; let stand 5 minutes. In a large bowl, combine cottage cheese, honey, egg, oil and salt.

Beat at medium speed with an electric mixer until blended. Add yeast mixture and 2 cups bread flour, beating until smooth. Gradually stir in whole-wheat flour, wheat germ, rye flour and oats. Add enough remaining bread flour to make a soft dough. Knead dough on a lightly floured surface until smooth and elastic. Place in a greased bowl; cover and let rise one hour or until double in bulk. Punch dough down. Shape into one round loaf and place in a pie pan coated with non-stick vegetable spray and sprinkled with cornmeal. Cover with greased plastic wrap and let dough rise again until double in bulk. Brush with egg white and sprinkle with sunflower kernels. Bake at 350 degrees for 35 to 40 minutes. Cool on a wire rack. Makes 6 to 8 servings.

Margaret Scoresby
Mosinee, WI

Olliebollen (Doughnuts)

114

DANISH SPICE COOKIES

You will start a new tradition with these cookies.

2 c. sifted all-purpose flour
1 t. cinnamon
1/2 t. salt
1/4 t. baking soda
1/4 t. ground cloves
1/2 c. butter or margarine
1 c. brown sugar, packed
1/2 c. sour cream
1 egg
1 t. vanilla extract
1 c. chopped dates
1/2 c. chopped walnuts

Sift flour, cinnamon, salt, baking soda and cloves in a bowl. Melt butter in a medium-sized saucepan; remove from heat. Add sugar and beat with a wooden spoon until combined. Beat in sour cream, egg and vanilla until smooth. Stir in flour mixture until thoroughly combined. Stir in dates and nuts. Spread evenly into a greased 15"x10"x1" pan. Bake at 350 degrees for 30 minutes or until top springs up. Makes 4 dozen.

Jennifer Muller

Little bars of fragrant goodness, Danish Spice Cookies get a flavor boost from an unexpected ingredient…sour cream! And when it comes to getting lots of zing for a minimum of fuss, you can't beat Bar Harbor Cranberry Pie.

Bar Harbor Cranberry Pie

START A NEW TRADITION: SHARE THE SEASON'S BOUNTY OF SWEETS WITH AN ELDERLY NEIGHBOR! DELIVER A BASKET OF COOKIES & A DINNER INVITATION.

BAR HARBOR CRANBERRY PIE

Frozen berries can also be used…no need to thaw before preparing this pretty pie.

2 c. cranberries
1 1/2 c. sugar, divided
1/2 c. chopped pecans
2 eggs, beaten
1 c. all-purpose flour
1/2 c. butter, melted
1/4 c. shortening, melted
Garnish: whipped cream and
    cinnamon (optional)

Lightly butter a 9" glass pie plate; spread cranberries over bottom. Sprinkle evenly with 1/2 cup sugar and pecans; set aside. In a separate bowl, add eggs and remaining one cup sugar; mix well. Blend in flour, butter and shortening; beat well after each addition. Pour over cranberries; bake at 325 degrees for 55 to 60 minutes. Garnish each serving with a dollop of whipped cream and a sprinkle of cinnamon, if desired. Serves 8.

Jean Hayes
La Porte, TX

Taste Tempting TReATS

Visions of sugarplums will dance in your head when you start whipping up these sensational sweets. A perfect ending to holiday meals or a special anytime snack, this collection of cookies, cakes, pies and more will satisfy any sweet tooth. The taste-tempting treats are also ideal to make for office parties or church potlucks.

Mini Christmas Cheesecakes

MINI CHRISTMAS CHEESECAKES

These look so pretty on your dessert table.

3 8-oz. pkgs. cream cheese, softened
1 1/2 c. sugar, divided
5 eggs
1 1/2 t. vanilla extract
1 c. sour cream
2 cans cherry pie filling

Beat together cream cheese and one cup sugar. Add eggs, one at a time, beating well after each addition. Add vanilla and mix again. Pour into mini foil cups, filling 3/4 full. Bake 20 minutes at 350 degrees. Remove from oven; let stand 5 minutes. Combine sour cream and remaining 1/2 cup sugar. Top each mini-cake with 1/2 teaspoon of the mixture and return to the oven for 5 minutes. When cooled, top each cheesecake with one cherry and a little of the filling. Keep refrigerated. Makes 8 dozen.

Mom's Gingerbread Cookies

MOM'S GINGERBREAD COOKIES

(Recipe used for cookies on front cover.)
When I was little, Mom and I used to bake gingerbread men together at Christmas time. I remember peeking through the oven door, waiting for one of them to get up off the pan, just like the story!

1/2 c. shortening
2 1/2 c. all-purpose flour, divided
1/2 c. sugar
1/2 c. molasses
1 egg
1 t. baking soda
1 t. ground ginger
1/2 t. cinnamon
1/2 t. ground cloves
candy-coated chocolate pieces

Beat shortening until softened. Add about 1 1/4 cups flour and next 7 ingredients. Beat until thoroughly combined. Stir in remaining 1 1/4 cups flour. Divide dough in half. Cover dough and chill for 3 hours or until easily handled. Roll each half of the dough to a 1/8" to 1/4" thickness. Cut out 4 1/2"-high cookies with gingerbread man cookie cutter. Place on ungreased baking sheets and bake at 375 degrees for 7 to 8 minutes or until edges are firm. Decorate with powdered sugar frosting and candies. Makes 2 dozen.

Powdered Sugar Frosting:
1 c. powdered sugar
1/4 t. vanilla extract
1 T. milk

Combine all ingredients, stirring until smooth. Transfer frosting to a pastry bag fitted with a small round tip. Pipe frosting onto cookies. Makes 1/3 cup.

Michele Urdahl
Litchfield, MN

Amazing DOUBLE CHOCOLATE TRUFFLES

..TRY MAKING FLAVORED TRUFFLES BY STIRRING IN DIFFERENT EXTRACTS...A TEASPOON OF ORANGE, PEPPERMINT OR RASPBERRY EXTRACT WILL DO THE TRICK.

6 1-OZ. SQS. SEMI-SWEET BAKING CHOCOLATE, CHOPPED
2 T. BUTTER
1/4 C. WHIPPING CREAM
12-OZ. PKG. WHITE CHOCOLATE CHIPS
2 T. SHORTENING
OPTIONAL: CHOPPED NUTS OR COLORFUL SPRINKLES

MELT BAKING CHOCOLATE IN A HEAVY SAUCEPAN OVER LOW HEAT, STIRRING CONSTANTLY; REMOVE FROM HEAT. ADD BUTTER AND WHIPPING CREAM; STIR 'TIL SMOOTH. REFRIGERATE FOR ONE HOUR. ROLL MIXTURE INTO ONE-INCH BALLS; PLACE ON AN ALUMINUM FOIL-LINED BAKING SHEET. FREEZE FOR 4 HOURS.
MELT WHITE CHOCOLATE CHIPS AND SHORTENING OVER LOW HEAT, STIRRING 'TIL SMOOTH. DIP FROZEN TRUFFLES INTO WHITE CHOCOLATE ~ RETURN TO BAKING SHEET. ROLL IN NUTS OR SPRINKLES, IF DESIRED. REFRIGERATE TRUFFLES FOR 10 TO 15 MINUTES 'TIL COATING IS SET. STORE IN AIRTIGHT CONTAINER. MAKES ONE DOZEN.

PRALINE SHORTBREAD COOKIES

It just isn't Christmas at our house without these cookies!

1 1/2 c. butter, softened and divided
3 c. powdered sugar, divided
2 c. all-purpose flour
1 c. pecans, finely chopped
1 T. plus 1/2 t. vanilla extract, divided
1 c. brown sugar, packed
1/8 t. salt
1/2 c. evaporated milk

Beat together one cup butter and one cup powdered sugar. Add flour, stirring until well blended. Stir in pecans and one tablespoon vanilla. Shape into one-inch balls and place 2 inches apart on ungreased baking sheets. Make an indentation in center of each cookie. Bake at 375 degrees for 15 minutes; do not brown. Cool on wire racks. In saucepan, melt remaining 1/2 cup butter. Add brown sugar and salt; bring to a boil for 2 minutes, stirring constantly. Remove from heat, stir in evaporated milk and return to heat. Once again, bring to a boil for 2 minutes. Remove from heat and allow mixture to cool to lukewarm. Stir in remaining 2 cups powdered sugar and remaining 1/2 teaspoon vanilla with a wooden spoon, stirring until smooth. Fill indentations in cookies with praline filling. Makes about 3 dozen.

Carol Hickman
Kingsport, TN

MEXICAN WEDDING COOKIES

A crunchy, classic cookie.

1 c. butter or margarine, softened
1/4 c. powdered sugar
1 t. almond extract
2 c. all-purpose flour
1/4 c. walnuts, finely chopped
powdered sugar

Beat first three ingredients until creamy. Stir in flour and nuts. Chill for a couple of hours. Make small balls and bake at 375 degrees for about 17 minutes. Cool a little and toss in powdered sugar. Makes about 2 1/2 dozen.

Amazing Double Chocolate Truffles

Chocolate-Coconut Sweeties

WHITE SUGAR COOKIES

My mother used this recipe for holidays and special treats when I was growing up.

5 c. all-purpose flour
5 t. baking powder
1 t. baking soda
1 t. salt
1 c. shortening
2 c. sugar
2 eggs
2 t. vanilla extract
$\frac{1}{4}$ t. nutmeg
$\frac{3}{4}$ c. milk

Combine flour, baking powder, baking soda and salt; set aside. In a large mixing bowl, beat shortening and sugar together. Beat in eggs, vanilla and nutmeg. Add milk alternately with dry ingredients, mixing well after each addition. Chill dough for at least 2 hours. Using approximately $\frac{1}{4}$ of the dough at a time, roll out on floured surface to $\frac{1}{4}$" thickness; cut out with cookie cutters. Bake at 350 degrees for 7 to 9 minutes on an ungreased baking sheet. When cooled, frost with vanilla frosting. Makes about 6$\frac{1}{2}$ dozen.

Vanilla Frosting:
3 c. powdered sugar
$\frac{1}{3}$ c. shortening
3 T. whipping cream or milk
1 T. margarine, softened
1$\frac{1}{2}$ t. vanilla extract
food coloring

Beat together all ingredients except food coloring. Frosting can be divided to make several different colors with food coloring. Spread frosting on cookies.

Sharon Lafountain

CHOCOLATE ♥ COCONUT SWEETIES
... they won't last long in the cookie jar!

1 c. BUTTER OR MARGARINE, SOFTENED
1 c. POWDERED SUGAR
$\frac{1}{2}$ t. SALT
1 t. VANILLA EXTRACT
2 c. ALL-PURPOSE FLOUR

... a recipe from
BRENDA DONLEY
♥ LAKE ISABELLA, MI

SWEETIES

BEAT BUTTER OR MARGARINE 'TIL FLUFFY; BEAT IN POWDERED SUGAR, SALT & VANILLA. GRADUALLY ADD FLOUR, BEATING WELL. COVER AND CHILL 8 HOURS. SHAPE INTO ONE-INCH BALLS. USING YOUR THUMB, GENTLY MAKE DEPRESSION IN CENTER OF EACH BALL; PLACE ON UNGREASED BAKING SHEETS. BAKE AT 350 DEGREES FOR 12 TO 15 MINUTES. SPOON A TEASPOON OF FILLING INTO EACH DEPRESSION WHILE WARM; DRIZZLE WITH FROSTING WHEN COOL. MAKES 4 DOZEN.

FILLING:
6 OZ. CREAM CHEESE, SOFTENED
2 c. POWDERED SUGAR
$\frac{1}{4}$ c. ALL-PURPOSE FLOUR
2 t. VANILLA EXTRACT
1 c. CHOPPED WALNUTS
1 c. SWEETENED FLAKED COCONUT

Combine all ingredients.

FROSTING:
1 c. SEMI-SWEET CHOCOLATE CHIPS
$\frac{1}{4}$ c. BUTTER OR MARGARINE
$\frac{1}{4}$ c. WATER
1 c. POWDERED SUGAR

Microwave chips, butter and water in a one-quart glass bowl on HIGH for one minute or 'til it melts. Gradually whisk in sugar 'til smooth & creamy.

Cream-Filled Pumpkin Roll

CREAM-FILLED PUMPKIN ROLL

You can make this beautiful dessert...it's easier than you think!

1 c. sugar
3/4 c. all-purpose flour
1 t. baking powder
1 t. cinnamon
1/8 t. salt
3 eggs, beaten
2/3 c. unsweetened canned pumpkin
3 T. powdered sugar, divided

Butter a 15"x10" jelly-roll pan; line with wax paper. Butter the wax paper; set aside. Mix together first 5 ingredients; blend in eggs and pumpkin. Spread batter in prepared pan. Bake at 375 degrees for 12 to 15 minutes or until center tests done. Lay a kitchen towel down on a flat surface and sprinkle 2 tablespoons powdered sugar over top. Cut around sides of pan to loosen cake; invert onto sugared towel, wax paper-side up. Fold one side of towel over one long side of cake and roll up jelly-roll style. Cool cake completely. Unroll cake and leave on towel; peel off wax paper. Spread filling evenly over cake. Use towel to help roll up cake and place seam side-down on a serving platter. Trim ends of cake; cover and refrigerate until ready to serve. Dust cake with remaining one tablespoon powdered sugar. Serves 8 to 10.

Cream Cheese Filling:
8-oz. pkg. cream cheese, softened
1 c. powdered sugar
2 T. unsalted butter, softened
1 t. vanilla extract
Optional: 1/2 c. chopped walnuts, toasted

Combine cream cheese, powdered sugar, butter and vanilla; blend well. Stir in walnuts, if desired.

Susan Greeves
Frederick, MD

WARM TURTLE CAKE

A cake that reminds me of the boxes of chocolate-covered turtles that my dad used to bring home for us when we were little!

18 1/4-oz. pkg. Swiss chocolate cake mix
1/2 c. plus 1/3 c. evaporated milk, divided
3/4 c. butter, melted
14-oz. pkg. caramels, unwrapped
1 c. chopped pecans
3/4 c. chocolate chips

Beat cake mix, 1/3 cup evaporated milk and melted butter on medium speed with an electric mixer for 2 minutes. Pour half of mixture into a greased 11"x7" baking pan. Bake at 350 degrees for 6 minutes. In a double boiler or microwave, melt caramels in the remaining 1/2 cup evaporated milk. Drizzle over cake. Sprinkle pecans and chocolate chips over caramel mixture. Use a wet knife to spread the remaining cake mixture over the pecan pieces and chocolate chips. Bake at 350 degrees for 18 minutes. Serves 12.

Laurie Benham
Playas, NM

MINT CHOCOLATE CHIP CHEESE BALL

You'll love the flavor of this sweet cheese ball.

12-oz. pkg. mini semi-sweet chocolate chips
12-oz. pkg. peppermint candies, crushed
8-oz. pkg. cream cheese, softened
1 c. chopped pecans
chocolate sugar wafers

Blend chocolate chips, peppermint candies and cream cheese together; roll in pecans. Serve with chocolate sugar wafers. Makes 2 1/2 cups.

CHRISTMAS PIE

If you take this festive pie to a holiday party, be sure to take copies of the recipe...everyone will want one!

8-oz. pkg. cream cheese, softened
1/2 c. powdered sugar
1 1/2 c. frozen whipped topping, thawed
9-inch graham cracker crust
1 c. fresh raspberries
1 c. water, divided
1 c. sugar
3 T. cornstarch
1/2 3-oz. pkg. raspberry gelatin

Beat cream cheese and powdered sugar until smooth; fold in whipped topping. Spread in crust; set aside. Place raspberries and 2/3 cup water in a saucepan; simmer for 3 minutes. Whisk sugar, cornstarch and remaining 1/3 cup water in a small bowl until smooth; add to raspberry mixture. Boil one minute, whisking constantly. Remove from heat. Add gelatin, whisking until smooth. Cool 5 to 7 minutes; pour over cream cheese mixture. Refrigerate 8 hours or until firm. Serves 8.

Caroline Wildhaber
Dayton, OR

CHOCOLATE CHESS PIE

This recipe was passed down from my grandma; it's truly wonderful.

5-oz. can evaporated milk
1 1/2 c. sugar
2 eggs, beaten
1/4 c. butter, melted
3 T. baking cocoa
1 t. vanilla extract
1/8 t. salt
9-inch pie crust

Combine first 7 ingredients; pour into an unbaked pie crust. Bake at 350 degrees for 40 to 45 minutes or until set. Makes 8 servings.

Michele Jones
Houston, TX

PRALINE-CREAM CHEESE POUND CAKE

My favorite because it has a rich caramel flavor that satisfies my most urgent sweet tooth!

1 c. butter, softened
8-oz. pkg. cream cheese, softened
1 lb. brown sugar
1 c. sugar
5 eggs
3 1/2 c. cake flour
1/2 t. baking powder
1 c. milk
1 1/2 t. vanilla extract
1 c. chopped pecans

Beat butter and cream cheese until well blended. Beat in brown sugar and sugar, one cup at a time, beating until light and fluffy. Add eggs, one at a time, beating well after each addition. Sift flour and baking powder together and add to creamed mixture alternately with milk, beginning and ending with flour. Add vanilla and nuts; mix well. Pour into a greased and floured tube pan.

Bake at 300 degrees for 2 hours or until cake tests done. Cool in pan for 10 minutes, remove from pan and cool on wire rack. Spread with frosting. Serves 14.

Frosting:
3 c. sugar, divided
1/2 c. water
1 egg, beaten
1 c. milk
1/2 c. butter
1 t. vinegar
1/8 t. salt

Place 1/2 cup of sugar in a heavy skillet. Cook over low heat, stirring constantly until melted and brown. Add water and stir until dissolved. Add remaining 2 1/2 cups sugar. Mix egg with milk and stir into sugar mixture. Add butter, vinegar and salt. Cook to soft ball stage, 234 to 243 degrees on candy thermometer; cool. Beat until mixture reaches spreading consistency.

Vicki Jones
Rutherfordton, NC

Christmas Pie

CHRISTMAS MEMORY BOX
(shown on page 10)
- photo box (ours measures 11"x7¹/₄"x4¹/₂")
- assorted scrapbook papers
- spray adhesive
- typewriter key charms
- twine
- small frame
- craft glue
- color photocopy of a vintage postcard
- scrap of fabric
- ¹/₈" dia. hole punch
- ³/₈"w red ribbon
- adhesive foam dots
- small tag sticker
- resin "remember" sticker
- assorted buttons
- beaded snowflake stickers
- small snowflake stickers
- tag alphabet stickers

1. Working in a well-ventilated area, use spray adhesive to cover the box sides and lid with scrapbook papers.

2. Thread typewriter keys onto two lengths of twine; attach the twine ends to the sides of the frame opening. Cover the frame back with scrapbook paper. Glue the frame to the lid.

3. Tear the edges of the postcard photocopy. Tear a fabric piece slightly larger than the postcard. Punch holes in the corners and use ribbon to knot the postcard to the fabric piece. Use foam dots to attach the fabric to the lid.

4. Tie a short ribbon length through the hole in the tag sticker. Apply the resin sticker to the tag. Use foam dots to attach the tag to the lid.

5. Apply buttons and stickers randomly to the box lid.

GIFT TAG ORNAMENTS
(shown on page 11)
For each ornament, cut 2 same-size felt pieces. Decorate one side of each piece . . . glue on ribbons or lace, attach fabric or felt pieces using embroidery stitches, sew on buttons or charms or attach pictures. Add your personalization; then, tack fibers and ribbons to the top for the hanger. Glue the felt pieces together back-to-back.

ACCORDION-FOLD ALBUM
(shown on page 12)
Cut a 6"x25¹/₄" strip of artist's paper. At one end of the strip, fold a 1¹/₄" flap. Accordion-fold the rest of the strip into 6" squares. Add decorations and photographs to the pages, cover and flap. Leaving a 6" tail, attach a 22" ribbon length to the front cover with foam dots. Wrap the remaining ribbon end around the album; tie the ends at the flap to secure.

FRAMED RECIPE
(shown on page 14)
Cut cardboard to fit inside a frame. Mount pieces of vintage tea towels or tablecloths on the cardboard for a background (if you don't want to cut your towels or tablecloths, use a color photocopy of them). Add the recipe to the background; then, embellish the background with other memorabilia such as a photo, a crocheted doily, buttons, charms and tags. Insert the background into the frame.

THE 12 TAGS OF CHRISTMAS
(continued from page 19)
I Believe
(shown on page 16)
Don't feel comfortable handwriting a message on your tag? Just photocopy or trace the "Believe" pattern that we've provided on page 143 onto a vellum piece; then, use the vellum to make a pocket on the tag. The childhood photo framed with cardstock is sure to remind you to believe in Santa.

HAPPY HOLIDAYS
(shown on page 17)
Rifle through your stash of vintage postcards and you're sure to find just the right background for this tag. Machine sew a singed vellum pocket to the tag; then, add brads, embroidered snap tape and a second tag and you're ready to wish your best someone "Happy Holidays."

Ho Ho Ho
(shown on page 17)
Believe it or not, you don't have to know how to crochet to create this tag. The cute Santa hat embellishment is purchased! To add even more interest, paint a metal label holder and rough it up a little with sandpaper before attaching it to the tag. Use adhesive foam dots to attach the snowflake charms to the tag.

Magic Reindeer Mix
(shown on page 17)
Rudolph is sure to stop Santa's sleigh at your house to snack on the magical mix included with this tag. Sew cardstock and cellophane pieces together to make a pocket and fill the pocket with Magic Reindeer Mix (dry oatmeal and glitter). Print the saying below onto cardstock and use it to label the back of the tag. Attach the tag to a child's gift.

On Christmas Eve, sprinkle this magic reindeer mix on your lawn to guide Santa's reindeer to your rooftop. While Santa makes his delivery inside, Rudolph and his friends can have a snack.

Santa's Favorites
(shown on page 18)
This tag reminds us that Santa wants us all to be good boys and girls. Spell out some of the message by printing or stamping your words onto cardstock or paper; then, adhere them to the tag. "X" and "O" tiles and a "good" sticker complete the message. Finish by chalking the tag edges for an antique look.

Dear Santa
(shown on page 18)
A needle, thread, buttons and a thimble are sure to help Santa mend his suit in case of a rip. For a clever hanger, attach a suspender clip to the top of the tag. Thread ribbon through the clip and sew across the ribbon to secure. Add a small note to Santa using a miniature clothespin.

A Christmas Present
(shown on page 18)
Stamps, stickers and ribbons make this tag a present all by itself. Start by stamping a background on the tag and a Santa figure on white cardstock. Color Santa with colored pencils. Add ribbons and postage stamp stickers and use adhesive foam dots to adhere Santa to the tag.

Wishes
(shown on page 18)
A recycled piece of vintage-look wrapping paper provides the perfect backdrop for this tag. Apply Soft Flock® fibers to Santa's coat and hat to make them look extra soft. Metal embellishments held on with red ribbon and a shiny tinsel hanger make it unique.

Family
(shown on page 18)
Create this tag in honor of your loved ones. Use a label maker to make a red tape that says "Christmas." Add a second tag, stickers and a miniature wreath. (Attach the wreath with craft glue.) Be sure to align the holes in the tags so it's easy to add the ribbon.

Holiday Wishes
(shown on page 18)
Torn fabric pieces turn this tag into a holder for a second tag. How clever! Begin by tearing four 1"x2" pieces of red fabric. Overlapping the long edges of the fabric pieces slightly, arrange the pieces on a cardstock rectangle and machine sew around the outside edges of the strips. Glue the cardstock to the tag. Make and embellish a second tag and weave it through the fabric slits.

FLEECE & CHENILLE STOCKINGS
(shown on page 22)
- ½ yard of 60"w blue fleece
- assorted cream buttons
- ⅜ yard white chenille
- ⅞ yard of ½"w cream twill tape
- ⅝ yard of 60"w cream fleece
- tracing paper
- blue felt
- fabric glue
- ⅓ yard of 60"w light blue fleece
- ½ yard light blue chenille rickrack
- ½ yard light blue chenille
- ½ yard cream pom-pom trim
- 3 white chenille stems

Use a ½" seam allowance for all sewing.

Large Stocking
1. Use a photocopier to enlarge the pattern on page 156 to 197%. Using the enlarged pattern, cut two stocking pieces (one in reverse) from blue fleece.

2. Avoiding the seam allowance, sew buttons to the stocking front as desired. Matching the right sides and leaving the top edge open, sew the stocking pieces together and turn right side out.

3. For the cuff, matching the right sides and short edges, fold an 11"x20" white chenille piece in half. Sew the short edges together. Matching the wrong sides and raw edges, fold the cuff in half. Matching the raw edges and the seam in the cuff to the heel-side seam of the stocking, insert the cuff in the stocking. Sew the cuff to the stocking along the raw edges. Turn the cuff to the outside.

4. For the hanger, fold a 10" length of twill tape in half and tack the ends inside the stocking at the heel-side seam.

Medium Stocking
1. Use a photocopier to enlarge the pattern on page 156 to 165%. Using the enlarged pattern, cut two stocking pieces (one in reverse) from cream fleece.

2. Matching the right sides and leaving the top edge open, sew the stocking pieces together and turn right side out.

3. Using the pattern on page 153, cut the snowflake pieces from blue felt and glue them to the stocking front.

4. For the cuff, follow Step 3 of the **Large Stocking**, using a 9"x17" piece of light blue fleece. Glue a 16" length of rickrack around the cuff.

5. For the hanger, follow Step 4 of the **Large Stocking**, using a 9" length of twill tape.

(continued on page 124)

SMALL STOCKING

1. Use a photocopier to enlarge the pattern on page 156 to 144%. Using the enlarged pattern, cut two stocking pieces (one in reverse) from light blue chenille.

2. Matching the right sides and leaving the top edge open, sew the stocking pieces together and turn right side out.

3. For the cuff, follow step 3 of the **Large Stocking** (page 123) using an 8"x15" piece of cream fleece; do not turn the cuff to the outside.

4. Pull the cuff out of the stocking. Glue a 14½" length of pom-pom trim along the folded edge and fold the cuff to the outside.

5. For the snowflake on the cuff, twist the chenille stems together at the center and curl the ends. Glue the snowflake to the center of one side of the cuff. Sew buttons to the cuff as desired.

6. For the hanger, follow Step 4 of the **Large Stocking**, using a 9" length of twill tape.

SNOWMAN CHAIRBACK COVER
(shown on page 24)
- ⅞ yard of 60"w white fleece
- cardboard
- polyester fiberfill
- upholstery needle and heavy-duty thread
- two ½" dia. black shank buttons
- tracing paper
- scraps of black and orange felt
- fabric glue
- blush and applicator
- ¼ yard red felt
- three 1" dia. tan pom-poms
- ½ yard white pom-pom fringe
- ½ yard light blue chenille rickrack
- child's round-back wooden chair
- white decorative yarn
- string
- fabric marking pen
- thumbtack
- 14"x17" watercolor paper
- 14"x17" piece of light blue felt
- stapler
- 1¼" dia. foam brush
- tan acrylic paint
- 1¾" dia. white pom-pom
- ⅝ yard red chenille rickrack

Our chairback cover was made for a 13½"wx15"h chairback. You may need to adjust the size of your cover to fit your chair.

1. Use a photocopier to enlarge the snowman body pattern on page 147 to 241%. Enlarge the snowman base pattern to 252%. Using the enlarged body pattern, cut the snowman back from white fleece. Extending the bottom edge 5", use the pattern and cut the snowman front from white fleece. Using the enlarged base pattern, cut a base from cardboard.

2. Matching the right sides and top edges and stopping ½" from the bottom edge of the snowman back, use a ½" seam allowance and sew the snowman front and back together. Sew a ½" hem along the raw edges. Turn right side out.

3. Insert the base in the snowman. Stuff the snowman's face. Sewing through both fleece layers and the base, sew the buttons to the face for eyes. Pull the thread tight to tuft the face and knot the ends.

4. Using the patterns, cut eyebrows, a mouth and a nose from felt. Matching the right sides, use a ¼" seam allowance and sew the sides of the nose together. Turn the nose right side out and stuff. Glue the nose, eyebrows and mouth to the face. Blush the "cheeks."

5. For the snowman's buttons, glue three 1½" diameter red felt circles and the tan pom-poms to the body as shown. Glue a 15½" length each of pom-pom fringe and light blue rickrack to the bottom edge of the snowman front as shown.

6. Place the snowman over the chairback, resting the base on the back of the chair seat. Stuff the snowman's "belly."

7. For the scarf, cut a 3¾"x41" red felt piece and make 2½" long cuts, ¼" apart, along both ends for the fringe. Glue yarn stripes on the scarf. Tie the scarf around the snowman's "neck."

8. For the hat, tie one end of a length of string to the fabric pen. Insert the thumbtack through the string 13" from the pen. Insert the thumbtack in one corner of the watercolor paper. Holding the tack in place and keeping the string taut, mark the cutting line (See Fig. 1 of *Making a Fabric Circle* on page 142). Repeat on the light blue felt with the thumbtack 13¾" from the pen. Cut both pieces along the cutting lines.

9. Roll the paper hat into a cone and staple to secure. Overlapping and wrapping to the inside as necessary, use glue to cover the hat with the felt. Paint dots on the hat. Glue the white pom-pom and red rickrack to the hat as shown and place it on the snowman's head.

GIFT TAGS
(shown on page 24)
- small, medium and large tag dies and a die-cutting tool
- light blue, tan and textured cream cardstock
- white and blue polka-dot, red and white polka-dot, blue striped and red and white mesh-print scrapbook papers
- craft glue
- brown ink pad
- red thread
- light blue chipboard monogram
- $1/4$"w red ribbon
- snowflake charms
- alphabet rub-ons and stamps
- red staples and stapler
- red jute
- $3/16$"w and $1/2$"w red rickrack
- black fine-point permanent pen
- white wired pom-pom trim
- silver ball chain with connector

MONOGRAM TAG
Layer and glue die-cut cardstock and paper tags together as desired. Ink, then sew along the tag edges. Decorate the tag with the monogram, ribbon, charm and rub-ons. Cut out each word of a stamped message, ink the edges and staple them along one edge. Knot jute, ribbon and $3/16$"w rickrack through the hole in the tag.

TIP: If you don't have red staples, use a red permanent pen to color plain staples.

NOEL TAG
Glue die-cut light blue and cream cardstock tags together. Cut a paper pocket for the tag and glue a paper strip and $1/2$"w rickrack along the top. Sew along the tag edges, attaching the pocket to the tag. Decorate the tag with ink, cardstock, rub-ons, jute and a charm. Make one small and one medium layered cardstock and paper tag. Ink the tags and use rub-ons and the pen to add messages. Knot trim and attach

the chain through the holes in the tags. Place the smaller tags in the pocket on the large tag.

PEACE ON EARTH CARD
(shown on page 26)
- cream and light blue cardstock
- brown plaid scrapbook paper
- craft knife and cutting mat
- craft glue
- deckle-edged craft scissors
- snowflake punch
- mica flakes
- alphabet rub-ons
- 4" length each of $3/8$"w brown velvet ribbon and $3/8$"w brown rickrack

1. For the card, matching the short edges, fold a $5^{1}/2$"x8" cream cardstock piece and a $3^{7}/8$"x8" paper piece in half. Cut a 2" square opening in the center front of the paper, $1/2$" from the top edge.

2. Matching the folds and top edges, glue the cardstock and paper together; trim the sides with craft scissors. Cut a $1^{3}/4$" square opening in the cardstock at the center of the paper opening on the card front.

3. Punch 3 snowflakes, $5/8$" apart, in the center bottom of the card front. Set one punched snowflake aside. Apply glue to the cardstock. Sprinkle with mica flakes, allow to dry and shake off the excess.

4. Matching the short edges, fold a $5^{1}/2$"x8" light blue cardstock piece in half. Matching the folds, glue the cardstock inside the card.

5. Glue the punched snowflake to the cardstock in the center of the front opening. Use rub-ons to spell "peace on earth" in the opening. Glue mica flakes to the snowflake in spots.

6. Glue ribbon and rickrack to the card front over the bottom paper edge.

JOY CARD
(shown on page 26)
- light blue cardstock
- Thinkable Inkable™ Christmas stamp
- silver ink pad
- red and white ticking and polka-dot scrapbook papers
- craft glue
- deckle-edged craft scissors
- craft knife and cutting mat
- sandpaper
- silver wreath and alphabet charms
- red embroidery floss
- adhesive foam dots
- $3/16$" dia. silver brads

For the card, matching the short edges, fold a $4^{7}/8$"x$6^{1}/8$" cardstock piece in half. Stamp messages on the front. Matching the short edges, fold a $7/8$"x$6^{1}/8$" strip of ticking paper in half. Matching the folds, glue the strip to the card near one side edge. Trim the bottom front edge with craft scissors.

For the frame, cut a $2^{1}/2$"x$2^{7}/8$" polka-dot paper piece with a $1^{1}/2$"x$1^{7}/8$" opening at the center. Sand the frame edges. Knot the wreath charm onto the center of a 2" floss length and glue the floss ends to the back of one long frame edge. Attach the frame to the card front with foam dots. Use brads to attach the alphabet charms to the ticking paper.

STAMPED GIFT WRAP

(shown on page 26)
- 1¼" dia. foam brush
- light blue acrylic paint
- plain white gift wrap
- Thinkable Inkable™ Christmas stamp and assorted-sized alphabet stamps
- red ink pad
- red fine-point permanent pen
- light blue cardstock
- double-sided tape
- red and white polka-dot scrapbook paper
- packages
- red wired pom-pom trim
- adhesive foam dot
- large red pom-pom

Paint blue dots on the gift wrap; allow to dry. Stamp and write words and phrases on the gift wrap. Cut a cardstock tag. Tape the tag to the paper and cut the paper slightly larger than the tag. Stamp a message on the tag. Wrap the packages, tape the tag to the top package and tie the packages together with the trim. Use the foam dot to attach the large pom-pom to the top package.

GIFT BOX WITH SNOWFLAKE EMBELLISHMENT

(shown on page 26)
- gift box
- kraft paper
- double-sided tape
- assorted ribbons
- alphabet rub-ons
- black fine-point permanent pen
- tiny tag
- tiny silver bell
- red jute
- spray adhesive
- newsprint scrapbook paper
- 6" square of mat board
- tracing paper
- craft knife and cutting mat
- red wired pom-pom trim
- craft glue

Wrap the box with kraft paper. Tape ribbons around the box as desired. Use rub-ons to spell "Tis the Season" on some of the ribbons. Tie wide ribbon into a bow around one end of the box.

Write the recipient's name on the tag and tie the tag and bell onto one of the ribbons on the box with jute and narrow ribbon.

For the snowflake embellishment, working in a well-ventilated area, use spray adhesive to adhere the scrapbook paper to the mat board. Using the pattern on page 156, cut the snowflake from the mat board. Cut a length of trim with 8 pom-poms. Remove all but one pom-pom from the trim. Gluing the wired pom-pom to the top, glue the pom-poms to the tips of the snowflake. Use the wire to attach the snowflake to the wide ribbon bow.

CROSSWORD PUZZLE GIFT BAG

(shown on page 27)
- sandpaper
- blue gift bag without handles
- small and large scallop-edged craft scissors
- white paint pen
- white vellum
- vellum tape
- 9" length of ¼"w white ribbon
- craft glue
- white cardstock
- scrapbook paper (optional)
- ⅛" dia. hole punch
- alphabet rub-ons
- black fine-point permanent pen
- ¼" dia. blue brad

For a distressed look, sand the bag and wipe away the dust. Trim the top with the small scallop scissors. Paint dots and snowflakes on the bag. Photocopy the crossword puzzle on page 150 onto vellum; cut it out and tape it to the center of the bag front. Glue a ribbon bow to the corner of the puzzle.

Cut two 2⅜"x4" cardstock tags. If desired, cover one tag with paper. Punch a hole in the top of each tag and trim the bottom edges with the large scallop scissors. Use the rub-ons to spell "ACROSS" and "DOWN" on the tags as shown. Add the clues with the black pen. If desired, write the answers on the back of the tags. Attach the tags to the bag with the brad.

CROSSWORD PUZZLE CLUES

DOWN
1. December 25th
2. Let there be _____ on Earth
3. ____ log
5. Ebenezer _____
7. Hung by the chimney with care
8. A custom or ritual
12. Red-nosed reindeer
15. Holiday beverage
17. Four-letter word for Christmas

ACROSS
4. Three-letter word for happiness
6. Christmas bread
9. Saint Nick
10. A round door decoration
11. Rejoice, party, enjoy, make merry
13. When you ____ upon a star
14. Christmas flower
16. Famous snowman
18. Rhymes with jolly
19. Newborn king
20. Kiss under this

CROSSWORD PUZZLE ANSWERS

DOWN
1. Holiday
2. Peace
3. Yule
5. Scrooge
7. Stockings
8. Tradition
12. Rudolph
15. Eggnog
17. Noel

HO HO HO CARD

(shown on page 27)

- white and textured red cardstock
- black and red colored pencils
- craft glue
- two ⅝" dia. black shank buttons with the shanks removed
- 1¼" square silver buckle
- 1¼"x6" strip of black faux leather
- awl
- white decorative yarn
- alphabet dies and a die-cutting tool
- iridescent glitter
- adhesive foam dots

For the card, fold a 6"x12" red cardstock piece in half, matching the short edges. For the coat opening, draw a black line down the card front. Shade the front with the red pencil. Glue the buttons to the card front as shown. For the belt, slide the buckle onto the center of the leather strip. Use the awl to punch a hole in the strip for the buckle prong. Glue the belt to the card as shown. Glue yarn along the bottom edge of the card front. Die-cut "ho ho ho" from white cardstock. Apply glue to the letters. Sprinkle with glitter, allow to dry and shake off the excess. Use pieces of foam dots to adhere the letters to the card front.

WISH CARD

(shown on page 27)

- light blue and white cardstock
- blue and green harlequin-print and two-tone green-checked scrapbook papers
- craft glue
- spray adhesive
- mica flakes
- alphabet dies and a die-cutting tool
- iridescent glitter
- adhesive foam dots
- ⅛" dia. silver brads
- silver snowflake charms
- silver paint pen
- ¾ yard of ⅜"w blue-green ribbon

Use spray adhesive in a well-ventilated area.

For the card, fold a 6"x12" light blue cardstock piece in half, matching the short edges. Tear a 5½" white cardstock square and a 5¼" harlequin-print paper square. Glue the torn pieces together. Spray a torn 3"x4" white cardstock piece with adhesive. Sprinkle with mica flakes, allow to dry and shake off the excess. Glue the flaked cardstock to the center of the torn paper square. Die-cut "WISH" from checked paper. Using glue, apply glitter spots to the letters. Attach the letters to the flaked cardstock with foam dots. Use brads to attach charms to the layered pieces. Paint the edges of the card front. Glue the layered pieces to the card. Wrap ribbon around the card at the fold and tie the ends into a bow.

NATURALS

(shown on page 28)

WINDOW SWAG

Create this swag with real pine and cedar branches and pinecones or use artificial items for a decoration to use year after year. Use floral wire to join the pine and cedar branches together to form the swag. Accent the greenery with pinecones, white tallow berries, glitter sprays and white mica stars.

PEACE, LOVE AND HARMONY BASKETS

- hot glue gun
- floral foam
- 3 white-washed baskets
- large pinecones
- 3 small chalkboards and chalk
- matte spray sealer
- copper and green wire
- wire cutters
- cedar and pine branches
- white narcissus
- silver glitter sprays
- white tallow berries
- silver ornaments
- white mica stars

Use spray sealer in a well-ventilated area.

1. Hot glue floral foam inside each basket.

2. Hot glue pinecone scales around the edges of each chalkboard to form frames. Write "peace," "love" and "harmony" on the chalkboards, apply sealer and attach them to the front of each basket with wire and glue.

3. Arrange branches, narcissus and glitter sprays in each basket. Add pinecones, berries, ornaments and stars as shown.

(continued on page 128)

Twig Snowflakes

- twigs
- hot glue gun
- jute
- white acrylic paint
- paintbrush
- craft glue
- mica snow
- clear nylon thread

For each snowflake, cut or break 3 twigs into equal lengths. Arrange 2 of the twigs into an "X" and hot glue them together at the center. Hot glue the third twig across the center of the "X." Wrap jute around the center of the snowflake. For extra detail, hot glue smaller twigs to the snowflake. Brush thinned paint on the snowflake and allow to dry. Brush thinned glue on the snowflake. Sprinkle with mica snow, allow to dry and shake off the excess. Attach a thread hanger.

FROSTY

(continued from page 29)

Luminaries

Never leave burning candles unattended.

Glue glittered buttons on the wire handles of luminary jars. Brush glue over the jar lips and sprinkle with mica snow. Pour mica snow into the bottom of the jars, if you'd like, and add candles. Arrange the luminaries along the porch railing, light the candles and enjoy the glow.

Button Wreath Pillow

A bow of aqua ribbon and a circle of pearl buttons sewn to a plain red pillow add a quick & easy holiday touch to your décor.

Tufted Pillow

Sew a pearl button to the center of an aqua pillow, stitching through the entire pillow. Pull the thread tightly and tie at the back.

TRADITIONAL

(continued from page 33)

Rupert the Snowman

- protective gloves
- wire cutters
- 2 yards of 48"w heavy wire mesh screen
- heavy-duty stapler
- 8-gallon galvanized tub
- newspapers
- queen-size rolled batting
- dental floss
- hot glue gun
- tracing paper
- 7" square of orange felt
- 2 small black buttons
- 2 large black buttons
- spray adhesive
- mica flakes
- 1 yard of 72"w red felt
- 1/4 yard of 72"w white felt
- red embroidery floss
- holly sprig

Use a 1/2" seam allowance unless otherwise indicated.

1. Wearing the gloves, cut 1 1/3 yards from the screen. Spiral the screen into a loose cone shape with an 8" diameter bottom opening. Staple the cone closed at the top. Making sure the cone will fit inside the tub, staple the mesh together where it overlaps. Stuff the cone with crumpled newspapers to form the body and place in the tub.

2. Matching the short edges, shape and staple the remaining 2/3-yard screen into a tube. Place the bottom of the tube over the top of the body and staple in place. Stuff the tube with crumpled newspapers to form a rounded head. Fold the top end of the screen to the inside of the tube.

3. Cut batting long enough to go around the snowman. Wrap the batting around the body and head, stretching the batting slightly. Stitch the ends together at the back using dental floss. Tuck the batting at the bottom into the tub. Tie dental floss around the neck and tighten to emphasize the head.

4. Form 20-30 medium and 2 small batting snowballs. Hot glue the small snowballs to the snowman's face for cheeks. Hot glue the medium snowballs to the body, leaving 1"-2" between snowballs.

5. Stretch a large batting piece until it's thin. Starting at the neck, hot glue the batting over the snowballs, working down and tucking between snowballs for a lumpy effect. Repeat on the face and cheeks, using a smaller piece.

6. Using the pattern on page 151, cut the nose from orange felt. Matching the straight edges, stitch the sides together with a 1/4" seam allowance. Turn the nose right side out, stuff it with batting and hot glue it to the face.

7. For the eyes, hot glue a small button to the center of each large button. Hot glue the eyes to the face.

8. Working in a well-ventilated area, spray adhesive over the snowman and sprinkle with mica flakes. Spray again with adhesive to seal the mica flakes. Allow to dry overnight.

9. For the scarf, cut a 7"x60" red felt piece. Using the small diamond pattern on page 155, cut 6 white felt diamonds and hot glue to the scarf as shown. Using 6 strands of floss, refer to the photo to work *Running Stitches* (page 140) in a diamond pattern across the felt diamonds. Cut 1/2"x3" fringe strips at each end of the scarf before tying it around the snowman's neck.

10. For the hat, cut a 20" red felt square in half diagonally. Sew the pieces together along one long and one short edge; turn right side out.

11. For the brim, sew the short ends of a 6"x39" white felt piece together to form a loop. Matching the raw edges, fold the loop in half. Insert the loop inside the hat and sew the pieces together along the raw edges. Turn the brim to the outside and tack the holly to the edge. Hot glue a batting snowball to the tip of the hat.

ST. NICK
(shown on page 39)
BODY
- drill with ³/₄" and ¹/₈" bits
- 8¹/₂"x11¹/₂"x1" wood base
- 2"x2"x1" wood block
- two 36" lengths of ³/₄" dia. dowel rods
- wood tone spray
- craft glue
- 2 pairs of black socks
- polyester fiberfill
- 12 black buttons
- black and white embroidery floss
- 14-gauge galvanized craft wire
- wire cutters
- duct tape
- tissue paper
- XL red sweater
- white bulky weight novelty eyelash yarn
- white bulky weight brushed acrylic yarn
- size 17 (12.75 mm) knitting needles
- kraft paper
- black medium-point permanent marker

HEAD
- tissue paper
- mat board
- ¹/₄ yard peach cotton fabric
- air-soluble fabric marking pen
- polyester fiberfill
- 3" doll needle
- heavy-duty thread
- transfer paper

- #2 black Pigma® pen
- colored pencils
- white paint pen
- craft glue
- mohair fleece
- doll eyeglasses
- duct tape
- straight pins

Refer to Knit, page 141, before beginning the project, or use purchased trims for the collar, cuffs and hem.

BODY
1. Centering the holes lengthwise, drill two ³/₄" holes, 4" apart, in the base. Drill a ¹/₈" hole through the center of one side of the wood block and through each dowel, 5" from the top (Fig. 1).

Fig. 1

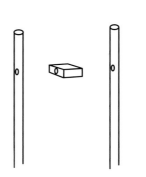

2. In a well-ventilated area, spray wood tone on the base. Securing with glue, insert the dowels in the holes (ends with holes are at the top). For boots, cut small slits in the heels of 2 socks and slip them over the dowels. Stuff the boots. Sew the buttons to the boots. Wrap black floss around the buttons in a crisscross pattern similar to lacing a shoe and tie a bow on each boot. Glue the bottom of the boots to the base.

3. Thread an 84" wire length through one dowel hole, the wood block and the remaining dowel. Even up the wire and bend each end into a "U." Tape the wire at the shoulders (Fig. 2).

Fig. 2

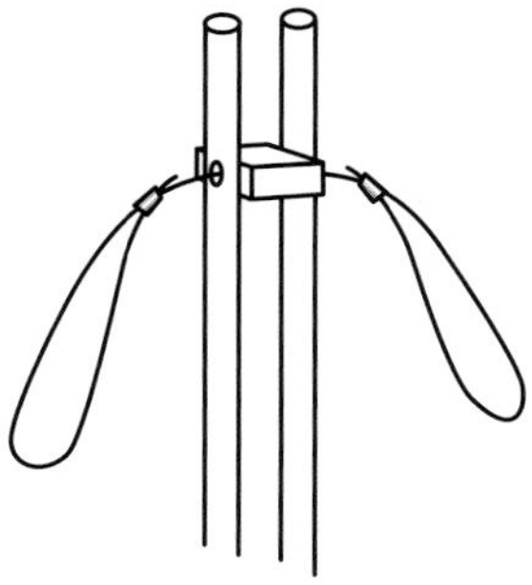

4. Enlarge the coat pattern on page 144, to 304% on a photocopier. Following *Making Patterns* on page 140, trace the pattern onto tissue. Unfold the tissue pattern. Turn the sweater wrong side out. Aligning the bottom pattern edge with the bottom sweater edge, pin the tissue pattern to the sweater through both layers. Machine zigzag along the pattern lines, leaving the bottom, collar and cuffs open. Tear the pattern away, cut ¹/₂" outside the stitching line and turn the coat right side out.

5. Holding the 2 yarns together, knit the following: a 4-stitch-wide by 15" long band for the fur collar, a 4-stitch-wide by 10¹/₂" long band for each fur sleeve cuff and a 7-stitch-wide by 25" long band for the bottom coat edge. Use white floss to *Whipstitch* (page 140) the bands to the coat.

6. Slip the coat over the dowel frame. For mittens, put a sock over each hand. Make a kraft paper list and glue it to the mittens.

HEAD
1. Trace the oval and face patterns from pages 144-145 onto tissue paper and cut them out. Using the pattern, cut an oval from mat board. Matching the right sides

(continued on page 130)

and short ends, fold the fabric in half. Use the fabric pen to draw around the face pattern on the fabric. Sew through both fabric layers along the profile line and leave the back open for turning. Cut away the fabric 1/4" outside the stitched profile and back lines and turn the face right side out. Sew *Running Stitches* 1/4" from the edge along the back opening. Firmly stuff the face, place the mat board in the back opening and pull and knot the threads to secure the opening around the mat board (Fig. 3).

Fig. 3

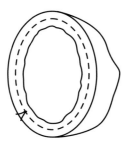

2. To sculpt the nose, follow the Nose Diagram and insert the doll needle through the top of the head, exiting at #1. Insert the needle next to #1. Digging deep into the stuffing and squeezing with your fingers to shape the nose, bring the needle up at #2. Insert the needle next to #2, dig deep and come up at #3. Continue until bringing the needle up at #9, insert diagonally and come up at #10. Insert the needle and come up at #11, gently squeezing the nostril into place. Insert diagonally from #11 to #12; return to #9. Stitch on the outside to #12. Come up at #11, then stitch on the outside to #10. Insert the needle into the fabric, exit through the top of the head and tie a knot.

Nose Diagram

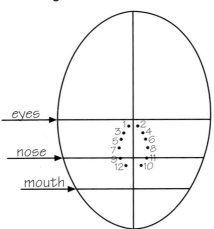

3. Transfer the eye patterns from page 144 onto the face. Outline with the Pigma pen. Color the eyes and cheeks with colored pencils. Paint the whites of the eyes and add highlights with the paint pen.

4. Glue mohair to the face as shown for the beard, mustache and eyebrows. Tack the earpieces of the glasses in place.

5. Tape the head to the top of the body and secure with pins. Follow **Santa's Hat Tree Topper** on page 39 to make the hat.

STRIPED KNIT STOCKING
(continued from page 37)
LEFT HEEL
Note: When instructed to slip a stitch, always slip as if to **purl**, unless otherwise instructed.

Row 1: Slip 9 sts onto st holder (Right Heel), slip next 18 sts onto second st holder (Top of Foot), slip 1, with Red knit across: 9 sts.

Row 2: Purl across.

Row 3: Slip 1, knit across.

Rows 4-9: Repeat Rows 2 and 3, 3 times.

Heel Turning: P1, P2 tog (Fig. 2, page 141), P1, **turn;** slip 1,

K2, **turn;** P2, P2 tog, P1, **turn;** slip 1, K3, **turn;** P3, P2 tog, P1, **turn;** slip 1, K4, **turn;** P4, P2 tog; cut yarn: 5 sts.

Slip remaining sts onto st holder.

RIGHT HEEL
With **right** side facing, slip 9 sts from Right Heel st holder onto empty needle.

Row 1: Holding two strands of Red together, knit across.

Row 2: Slip 1, purl across.

Row 3: Knit across.

Rows 4-8: Repeat Rows 2 and 3 twice, then repeat Row 2 once **more**.

Heel Turning: K1, K2 tog (Fig. 1, page 141), K1, **turn;** slip 1, P2, **turn;** K2, K2 tog, K1, **turn;** slip 1, P3, **turn;** K3, K2 tog, K1, **turn;** slip 1, P4, **turn;** K4, K2 tog: 5 sts.

GUSSET AND INSTEP
Row 1: With **right** side facing, pick up 4 sts along side of Right Heel (Fig. 4, page 141), slip 18 sts from Top of Foot st holder onto an empty needle and knit across, pick up 4 sts along side of Left Heel, knit 5 sts from Left Heel st holder: 36 sts.

Row 2: Purl across.

Row 3: Holding one strand of **each** White together, K8, K2 tog, K 16, slip 1 as if to **knit**, K1, PSSO (Figs. 3a & 3b, page 141), K8: 34 sts.

Row 4: Purl across.

Row 5: K7, K2 tog, K 16, slip 1 as if to **knit**, K1, PSSO, K7: 32 sts.

Row 6: Purl across.

Row 7: Holding two strands of Red together, K6, K2 tog, K 16, slip 1 as if to **knit**, K1, PSSO, K6: 30 sts.

Row 8: Purl across.

Row 9: Holding one strand of **each** White together, K5, K2 tog, K 16, slip 1 as if to **knit**, K1, PSSO, K5: 28 sts.

Row 10: Purl across.

Row 11: Knit across.

Row 12: Purl across.

Row 13: Holding two strands of Red together, knit across.

Row 14: Purl across.

Row 15: Holding one strand of **each** White together, knit across.

Rows 16-26: Repeat Rows 10-15 once, Rows 10-14 once **more**.

Cut White.

TOE SHAPING

Row 1: Holding two strands of Red together, K4, K2 tog, K1, place marker, K1, slip 1 as if to **knit**, K1, PSSO, K8, K2 tog, K1, place marker, K1, slip 1 as if to **knit**, K1, PSSO, K4: 24 sts.

Row 2: Purl across.

Row 3: ★ Knit across to within 3 sts of marker, K2 tog, K2, slip 1 as if to **knit**, K1, PSSO; repeat from ★ once **more**, knit across: 20 sts.

Row 4: Purl across.

Rows 5 and 6: Repeat Rows 3 and 4: 16 sts.

Bind off all sts.

FINISHING

With **right** sides together and beginning at Toe, weave seam to within 3¹/₂" (9 cm) from top edge (Fig. 5, page 141), with **wrong** sides together, weave remaining seam. Fold Cuff over.

Hanging Loop: Holding 2 strands of Red together, cast on 12 sts.

Bind off all sts in **knit**.

Sew to seam inside Cuff.

DOTTED KNIT STOCKING
(shown on page 37)
Refer to Knit, page 141, before beginning the project.

FINISHED SIZE: 7¹/₂"x31" (19x78.5 cm)

MATERIALS
Bulky Weight Yarn
 [5 ounces, 255 yards
 (140 grams, 232 meters)
 per skein]:
 Red - 2 skeins
Bulky Weight Novelty Eyelash Yarn
 [1³/₄ ounces, 47 yards
 (50 grams, 43 meters)
 per skein]:
 White - 2 skeins
Bulky Weight Brushed Acrylic Yarn
 [3¹/₂ ounces, 142 yards
 (100 grams, 129 meters)
 per skein]:
 White - 1 skein
Straight knitting needles, size 13
 (9 mm) **or** size needed for gauge
Stitch holders - 3
Yarn needle

GAUGE: Holding two strands of Red together, in Stockinette Stitch, 9 sts and 13 rows = 4" (10 cm)

CUFF
Holding one strand of **each** White together, cast on 36 sts.

Work in K1, P1 ribbing for 7" (18 cm).

Cut yarn.

LEG
Row 1 (Right side): Holding two strands of Red together, knit across.

Row 2: Purl across.

Row 3: Knit across.

Row 4: Purl across.

Rows 5-64: Repeat Rows 3 and 4, 30 times.

Cut yarn.

LEFT HEEL
Note: When instructed to slip a stitch, always slip as if to **purl**, unless otherwise instructed.

Row 1: Slip 9 sts onto st holder (Right Heel), slip next 18 sts onto second st holder (Top of Foot), slip 1, holding one strand of **each** White together, knit across: 9 sts.

Row 2: Purl across.

Row 3: Slip 1, knit across.

Rows 4-9: Repeat Rows 2 and 3, 3 times.

Heel Turning: P1, P2 tog (Fig. 2, page 141), P1, **turn**; slip 1, K2, **turn**; P2, P2 tog, P1, **turn**; slip 1, K3, **turn**; P3, P2 tog, P1, **turn**; slip 1, K4, **turn**; P4, P2 tog; cut yarn: 5 sts.

Slip remaining sts onto st holder.

RIGHT HEEL
With **right** side facing, slip 9 sts from Right Heel st holder onto empty needle.

Row 1: Holding one strand of **each** White together, knit across.

(continued on page 132)

Row 2: Slip 1, purl across.

Row 3: Knit across.

Rows 4-8: Repeat Rows 2 and 3 twice, then repeat Row 2 once **more**.

Heel Turning: K1, K2 tog (Fig. 1, page 141), K1, **turn**; slip 1, P2, **turn**; K2, K2 tog, K1, **turn**; slip 1, P3, **turn**; K3, K2 tog, K1, **turn**; slip 1, P4, **turn**; K4, K2 tog, cut yarn: 5 sts.

GUSSET AND INSTEP
Row 1: With **right** side facing, slip 5 sts onto left needle, holding two strands of Red together, K5, pick up 4 sts along side of Right Heel (Fig. 4, page 141), slip 18 sts from Top of Foot st holder onto an empty needle and knit across, pick up 4 sts along side of Left Heel, knit 5 sts from Left Heel st holder: 36 sts.

Row 2: Purl across.

Row 3: K8, K2 tog, K 16, slip 1 as if to **knit**, K1, PSSO (Figs. 3a & 3b, page 141), K8: 34 sts.

Row 4: Purl across.

Row 5: K7, K2 tog, K 16, slip 1 as if to **knit**, K1, PSSO, K7: 32 sts.

Row 6: Purl across.

Row 7: K6, K2 tog, K 16, slip 1 as if to **knit**, K1, PSSO, K6: 30 sts.

Row 8: Purl across.

Row 9: K5, K2 tog, K 16, slip 1 as if to **knit**, K1, PSSO, K5: 28 sts.

Row 10: Purl across.

Row 11: Knit across.

Row 12: Purl across.

Rows 13-26: Repeat Rows 11 and 12, 7 times.

Cut yarn.

TOE SHAPING
Row 1: Holding one strand of **each** White together, K4, K2 tog, K1, place marker, K1, slip 1 as if to **knit**, K1, PSSO, K8, K2 tog, K1, place marker, K1, slip 1 as if to **knit**, K1, PSSO, K4: 24 sts.

Row 2: Purl across.

Row 3: ★ Knit across to within 3 sts of marker, K2 tog, K2, slip 1 as if to **knit**, K1, PSSO; repeat from ★ once **more**, knit across: 20 sts.

Row 4: Purl across.

Rows 5 and 6: Repeat Rows 3 and 4: 16 sts.

Bind off all sts.

FINISHING
With **right** sides together and beginning at Toe, weave seam to within 3¹/₂" (9 cm) from top edge (Fig. 5, page 141), with **wrong** sides together, weave remaining seam. Fold Cuff over.

Hanging Loop: Holding 2 strands of Red together, cast on 12 sts.

Bind off all sts in **knit**.

Sew to seam inside Cuff.

Dots: Tack spirals of White Eyelash yarn to the stocking.

NEWSPRINT NOEL MANTELSCAPE
(shown on page 40)
MERRY CHRISTMAS BANNER
Use a computer to print "Merry Christmas;" then, enlarge the letters to the desired size with a photocopier. Cut out the letters and glue them to newsprint scrapbook paper squares. For the banner, evenly space and glue the squares onto 2 long strips of lightweight cardboard.

Folding between letters, accordion-fold each strip. Brush thinned glue over the banner edges. Sprinkle with mica snow, allow to dry and tap off the excess.

NEWSPRINT STARS
Adhere newsprint scrapbook paper to cardstock. Trace the pattern on page 145 onto tracing paper. Using the pattern, cut 2 stars from the covered cardstock. Refer to the pattern to accordion-fold each star along the dashed lines. Matching the wrong sides, glue the tips of the stars together.

WREATH
Wrap 1¹/₂" wide ribbon around a plain 20" diameter wreath. Referring to the photo, use floral wire to attach poinsettias, ornaments and flocked branches to the wreath. Tuck a few **Newsprint Stars** into the branches and hang the wreath in front of a mirror.

GARLAND
Swag the garland across the mantel. Insert flocked branches into the garland, add ornaments and attach a bow to each end. Finally, tuck a few **Newsprint Stars** here and there. You can also hang the garland across the top of a doorway or along the top of a china cabinet.

CHRISTMAS GARDEN MANTELSCAPE

(shown on page 41)
Use spray sealer in a well-ventilated area.

NOEL GATE SIGN

For the chalkboard embellishment, find a chalkboard to fit your gate or paint a wooden plaque with chalkboard paint. Write holiday wishes across the chalkboard with a white colored pencil; then, seal the chalkboard with matte spray sealer. Use a computer to print "NOEL;" then, enlarge the letters to fit on the chalkboard with a photocopier. Transfer the letters to the chalkboard. Allowing to dry between coats, paint the letters with crackle medium, then ivory acrylic paint. Add a second coat if necessary. Seal the chalkboard again. Wire the chalkboard and a **Distressed Tin Dove** to the gate.

GARLAND

Embellish a shell garland by dotting glue on the shells and sprinkling them with mica snow. Weave the garland across your mantel along with a beaded-leaf garland, greenery, candles and **Crackled Papier-Mâché Apples**.

DISTRESSED TIN DOVES

Refer to *Painting* on page 141 to *Dry Brush* 2 tin doves with ivory acrylic paint. Seal the doves with matte spray sealer. Wire the doves to the **Noel Gate Sign** and a **Distressed Obelisk**.

CRACKLED PAPIER-MÂCHÉ APPLES

Refer to *Painting* on page 141 to *Dry Brush* papier-mâché apples with burnt umber acrylic paint; allow to dry. Allowing to dry between coats, paint the apples with crackle medium, then green acrylic paint. Seal with matte spray sealer.

DISTRESSED OBELISKS

Refer to *Painting* on page 141 to *Dry Brush* each metal obelisk topiary form with ivory acrylic paint. Seal with matte spray sealer.

ENVELOPES

Use caution when placing items near an open flame.

For each envelope, cut a 7"x30" rectangle from textured wallpaper. Fold the rectangle into three 10" sections. Referring to Fig. 1, mark 2¼" above the bottom corners of the rectangle. Draw a line from each mark to the top corner of the center section and cut along the marked lines.

Fig. 1

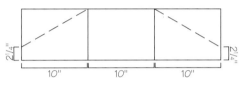

Refer to *Painting* on page 141 to *Dry Brush* burnt umber acrylic paint over the textured side of the wallpaper; allow to dry. Repeat with antique white acrylic paint. Cut an 8"x10" cotton fabric piece. Press one long fabric edge 1" to the back. With the pressed edge at the top, glue the fabric to the smooth side of the center wallpaper section. Fold the outside wallpaper sections to the center and glue along the bottom edge to form the envelope. Punch a hole in the upper right corner. For the hanger, fold an 18" ribbon length in half. Insert the ribbon ends through the hole and knot them together. Punch a hole in the lower left corner and attach a decorative tea ball.

LODGE-INSPIRED MANTELSCAPE

(shown on page 42)
SOCK-LIKE STOCKINGS

A red wool sweater, purchased at a thrift shop and felted, provides the fabric used for the details on these sock-like stockings. Felt could also be used, if desired.

- red wool sweater, felted
- fusible web
- red and grey embroidery floss
- corrugated cardstock
- alphabet stickers
- ¼" dia. hole punch
- twine

For each small stocking:
- ¼ yard cream textured fabric for stocking
- ¼ yard cream fabric for lining

For each large stocking:
- ⅔ yard green plaid flannel for stocking and lining

Use a ¼" seam allowance unless otherwise indicated.

Use a photocopier to enlarge the pattern on page 157 to 194% for the small stocking or 243% for the large stocking. For each stocking, cut 2 stocking pieces and 2 lining pieces from fabric (one each in reverse). Cut 2 toes and 2 heels (one each in reverse) and stripes from felted wool. Fuse the wool pieces to the stocking pieces. Referring to *Embroidery Stitches* on page 140, embroider the stocking as desired. Matching the right sides and leaving the top open, stitch the stocking pieces together; turn right side out. Repeat to sew the lining pieces together, leaving an opening for turning; do not turn the lining right side out. Matching the right sides and raw edges, place the stocking in the lining. For the hanger, fold a 2"x6" wool strip in half lengthwise and sew the long edges together. Matching the raw edges, place the

(continued on page 134)

hanger between the stocking and lining at the heel-side seam. Using a $\frac{1}{2}$" seam allowance, sew the pieces together along the top edges. Turn the stocking right side out through the opening in the lining and sew the opening closed. For each stocking, cut a corrugated cardstock tag, add a name with stickers and punch a hole at the top. Tie the tags to the stockings with twine.

Birch Twig-Wrapped Candles
Never leave burning candles unattended.

For each candle, use a rubber band to hold trimmed twigs in place around the candle. Tie twine around the twigs; remove the rubber band. Hang resin snowflakes from the twigs as desired.

Birch-Framed Cabin Art
- $11\frac{1}{4}$"x18" wooden board
- transfer paper
- wood burning tool
- color blending medium
- white, yellow, green, brown, grey, blue and red acrylic paints
- paintbrushes
- sawtooth picture hanger
- jigsaw
- moss-covered faux birch branches
- hammer & nails
- hot glue gun
- twine

Use caution when working with the wood burning tool. Allow paint to dry after each application.

Use a photocopier to enlarge the pattern on page 146 to 244%. Transfer the pattern to the front of the board. Use the round tip of the wood burning tool to outline the design. To add dots to the spokes of each snowflake, briefly hold the tip straight down. Mix thinned paint with blending medium to make a wash of each color. Paint

the design. Add an additional coat of white to the snow and smoke. Attach the hanger to the back of the board. Cut 2 branches each 18" and 24" long. Nail long branches to the long edges of the board. Glue short branches to the short edges of the board. Use twine to tie the short branches to the long branches at the intersections.

DREAMY MANTELSCAPE
(shown on page 43)
Wish Glitter Letters
- mat board
- craft knife and cutting mat
- silver and champagne-colored metallic acrylic paints
- paintbrushes
- craft glue
- silver and gold glitter
- 14-gauge wire
- wire cutters
- 1" dia. dowel rod
- four 4" square wooden blocks
- drill & small drill bit
- hot glue
- duct tape

Use caution when placing items near an open flame.

Use a computer to print "WISH;" then, use a photocopier to enlarge the letters to the desired size. Cut out the letters. Draw around the letters onto mat board; cut out. Alternating colors, paint the letters; allow to dry. Brush thinned glue onto the letters. Sprinkle silver glitter over the silver letters and gold glitter over the champagne-colored letters. Allow to dry; then, shake off the excess glitter. Coil 4 wire lengths around the dowel rod. Drill a hole in one side of each wooden block. Hot glue one end of each wire into a wooden block and duct tape a letter to the opposite wire end.

Glitter Stars
Use spray paint in a well-ventilated area.

Spray 3-dimensional papier-mâché stars with silver and gold spray paints; allow to dry. Brush thinned glue onto the stars. Sprinkle silver glitter over the silver stars and gold glitter over the gold stars. Allow to dry; then, shake off the excess glitter. Tuck some of the stars into the greenery on the mantel. Hot glue sheer ribbons to the backs of the remaining stars and hang them from the ceiling.

Mantel Candles
Use caution when placing items near an open flame. Never leave burning candles unattended.

For each candle, using the pattern on page 157, without the seam allowance, and repeating the pattern as necessary to fit around your candle, cut a red felt collar. Wrap the collar around the candle, overlapping the ends at the back and pinning them to the candle with a gold sequin pin. Thread a gold seed bead and sequin onto a gold sequin pin and insert the pin into the center of each scallop to secure the collar to the candle.

Tussie-Mussie "Stockings"
For each "stocking," you will need:
- $\frac{1}{3}$ yard brown linen
- $\frac{1}{3}$ yard cotton print for lining
- $\frac{1}{8}$ yard white felt
- tissue paper
- dark brown embroidery floss
- $\frac{1}{8}$ yard red felt
- fabric glue
- pre-strung silver sequins
- beaded snowflakes
- $\frac{3}{8}$" dia. silver sequins
- silver seed beads

Use a $\frac{1}{2}$" seam allowance for all sewing.

Use a photocopier to enlarge the pattern on page 143 to 285%. Using the pattern, cut one cone each from linen and lining fabric. Cut the band from white felt. Trace the embroidery pattern on page 149 onto tissue paper. Center the pattern on the band. Referring to *Embroidery Stitches* on page 140 and stitching through the tissue, follow the stitch key and embroider the design on the band using 3 strands of floss. Carefully tear away the tissue. Referring to the pattern for placement, zigzag the embroidered band to the linen cone piece. Repeating the pattern as needed, use the pattern on page 157 and cut a red felt scallop piece; sew the straight edge to the top of the linen cone piece. Fold each cone piece in half, matching the right sides and side edges. Sew the side edges together, leaving an opening in the side of the lining for turning. Clip the points and turn the linen cone right side out. Matching the right sides and top edges, place the linen cone in the lining cone. Sew the pieces together along the top edges for the stocking. Turn the stocking right side out through the opening in the lining and sew the opening closed. Topstitch around the top of the stocking $1/4$" from the edge.

For the hanger, fold a 2"x5" linen strip in half, matching the right sides and long edges; sew the long edges together. Turn the strip right side out and press with the seam at the center back. Turning the ends of the strip $1/2$" to the back, sew the hanger to the top back of the stocking. Glue the pre-strung sequins along the edges of the embroidered band. Tack the beaded snowflakes and sequins with seed beads in the center to the stocking.

CHOCOLATE-COVERED CHERRIES RECIPE TAG
(shown on page 47)
For each tag, use a computer to print the recipe on page 47 onto cream cardstock and cut it into a tag (we mixed fonts on our tag). Punch a hole at the top. Stamp "Chocolate-Covered Cherries" on the back and glue rickrack along one long edge. Knot red ribbons and jute through the hole. For the tag holder, cut a red cardstock piece wider than the tag. Arrange ribbon and fabric strips on the cardstock as shown. Sew along the side and bottom edges, securing the strips to the cardstock. Attach crocheted cherries to the corner of the holder with a brad. Insert the tag in the holder.

PERSONALIZED ORNAMENT BOX
(shown on page 48)
• $5/8$ yard floral print cotton fabric
• 11"x$7^1/2$"x$4^1/2$" photo box with lid
• spray adhesive
• fabric glue
• $2^1/8$ yards of 1"w red ribbon
• red, black, green and cream cardstock
• beige striped scrapbook paper
• tracing paper
• $1/4$" dia. red plastic snap
• alphabet rub-ons
• black fine-point permanent pen
• green, brown and red chalk
• $1/2$" dia. black pom-pom

Use spray adhesive in a well-ventilated area. Yardage is based on fabric with a 40" usable width.

Use spray adhesive to cover the box and lid with fabric. Glue ribbon over any raw edges. Cut a $6^7/8$"x$10^1/8$" red cardstock piece and tear a $6^5/8$"x10" black cardstock piece. Use spray adhesive to glue the pieces to the lid. Print the desired letter from a computer. Use a photocopier to enlarge the letter to the desired size and cut it out. Draw around

the letter on paper and cut it out. Using the patterns on page 151, cut flower and vine pieces from cardstock. Attach the snap to the top of a small green cardstock tag. Spell a name on the letter with rub-ons. Write "ornaments" on the tag. Chalk the edges of the tag, letter, flower and vine pieces. Glue the pieces on the lid as shown, gluing the flower petals at the center only. Glue the pom-pom to the center of the flower.

SNOWMAN TAG ORNAMENT
(shown on page 49)
• white frosted shrinkable plastic
• colored pencils
• black fine-point permanent pen
• $3/16$" and $1/4$" dia. hole punches
• wire cutters
• 24-gauge blue wire
• red, green and blue beads
• jewelry pliers
• $7^3/4$" length of $1/4$"w sheer white ribbon
• craft glue
• white cardstock
• red and white striped scrapbook paper

Trace the patterns on page 145 onto the frosted side of the plastic and color with colored pencils. Draw over the face with the pen. Cut the pieces out and punch $3/16$" diameter holes as indicated on the patterns. Follow the manufacturer's instructions to bake. Connect the body and leg pieces with wire. Cut a 13" wire length for the arms and top loop. Attach one end to the snowman and thread one mitten, beads and the remaining mitten onto the wire, using pliers to curl the wire as shown. Attach the remaining end to the opposite side of the body. Glue the ribbon ends to the back of the head for a hanger. Glue $2^5/8$"x$4^3/4$" cardstock and paper tags together; punch a $1/4$" diameter hole in the top. Thread the hanger through the hole and spot glue the head to the tag.

SANTA CARD ORNAMENT

(shown on page 49)

Cover a tabbed index card with scrapbook papers and ribbon. Adhere foil tape along the edges. Add a Santa image, vellum messages and a wooden disk with a rub-on initial. Use wire and alphabet beads to spell "Santa" on a "Handmade by" label. Decorate the card with crocheted leaves, buttons, charms and a paperclip. Knot wide ribbon through a suspender clip attached to the tab.

PINK & BROWN CARD SET

(shown on page 50)
- double-sided solid/printed scrapbook papers
- scallop-edged craft scissors
- alphabet rub-ons
- tracing paper
- cream linen-print scrapbook paper
- craft glue
- $1/4$"w ribbon
- recycled clear plastic package (ours measures $3^5/8$"x$1^3/4$"x$5^3/8$")
- paper shreds
- colored pencil
- $1^5/8$"w sheer ribbon
- star charm with jump ring
- stem with leaves and berries

For each card, matching the solid side and short edges, fold a $2^5/8$"x8" double-sided paper piece in half. Cut away $3/8$" of the front short edge with the craft scissors. Use rub-ons to spell a name on the card front.

For each envelope, use the pattern on page 150 and cut an envelope from cream paper. Fold the side and bottom flaps to the back as indicated by the dashed lines on the pattern and glue them together where they overlap. Glue a $5/8$"w double-sided paper strip trimmed with the craft scissors along the bottom edge of the envelope flap as shown.

Stack the cards and envelopes and tie $1/4$"w ribbon around them. Trim the front and side edges of the package with the craft scissors. Place paper shreds, the cards and envelopes and the colored pencil in the package. Wrap sheer ribbon around the package. Attach the charm to the ribbon and tie the ribbon ends into a bow. Tuck the stem behind the bow.

INITIAL CARD SET

(shown on page 51)
- tan cardstock
- large scallop-edged craft scissors
- tan and black striped and floral scrapbook papers
- craft glue
- 4"x$5^1/2$" cream cards with pointed-flap envelopes
- black paint pen
- clear dimensional glaze
- $1/4$"w black satin ribbon
- large red beads

For each card, use a computer to print a letter on cardstock and trim the cardstock to $2^1/2$"x3" with the letter at the center. Using the craft scissors on the long edges, cut a 2"x$5^1/2$" striped paper strip. Cut a $1^1/2$"x$5^1/2$" floral paper strip. Glue the paper strips and letter to the card as shown. Paint dots on the card front.

For each envelope, print the letter on cardstock at a smaller point size. Cut the cardstock into a 1" diameter circle with the letter at the center. Apply glaze to the circle and allow to dry. Glue the top half of the circle to the point of the envelope flap.

Stack the cards and envelopes and tie ribbon into a bow around them. Being careful not to get glue on the cards, glue beads to the bow.

BOXED GREEN & BROWN STATIONERY SET

(shown on page 53)
- textured green cardstock
- craft glue
- multi-color striped, multi-color dotted, yellow dotted, pink alphabet and brown pin-striped scrapbook papers
- $1/8$"w pink and white polka-dot ribbon
- $1^1/2$" and $1^1/4$" dia. circle punches
- alphabet stamps
- brown ink pad
- $5^1/2$" square white envelopes
- $6^3/4$"x$6^3/4$"x$5/8$" gift box with lid
- die-cutting tool and a $3^1/4$"-tall tag die
- vellum quote
- deckle-edged craft scissors
- $1/8$" dia. pewter brads
- $7/8$ yard of 1"w green grosgrain ribbon

For each note card, cut a $5^1/4$" cardstock square. Layer and glue a $3/8$"x$5^1/4$" multi-color striped paper piece, a torn $7/8$"x$5^1/4$" multi-color dotted paper strip and a $5^1/4$" polka-dot ribbon length on the note card, $3/8$" from the top edge. Punch a $1^1/2$" diameter circle from yellow dotted paper and a $1^1/4$" diameter circle from alphabet paper. Layer and glue the circles on the center of the layered strips. Stamp a monogram on the circles.

Glue a multi-color striped paper piece to each envelope flap. Stack the envelopes and tie an 18" polka-dot ribbon length around them; repeat for the cards.

Trimming the paper corners as necessary, cover the inside of the box with pin-striped paper, the outside of the box with multi-color striped paper and the outside of the lid with multi-color dotted paper. Glue a $27^1/2$" polka-dot ribbon length along the top edges of the box.

Die-cut a tag from pin-striped paper. Trim the vellum quote with the craft scissors and attach it to the tag with brads. Layer and glue a 9¼" length each of grosgrain and polka-dot ribbon together. Tie an 18" length each of grosgrain and polka-dot ribbon into a bow around the center of the layered length. Tie the tag onto the center of the bow with a 4" polka-dot ribbon length. Wrapping the ends to the inside, center and glue the layered length across the lid. Place the envelopes and note cards in the box.

BOXED PERSONALIZED CARD SET
(shown on page 53)
- double-sided floral/light green scrapbook paper
- small scallop-edged craft scissors
- white vellum
- pink cardstock
- double-sided tape
- ⅛" dia. hole punch
- ¼"w green sheer ribbon
- tracing paper
- craft glue
- tissue paper
- 4"x4"x1¼" white gift box with lid
- black fine-point permanent pen
- 1"-tall tag
- white embroidery floss
- ⅜"w green ribbon
- snowflake charms

For each card, matching the light green side and short edges, fold a 3½"x7½" paper piece in half. Trim ¼" from the bottom front edge with the craft scissors.

Using a computer, type a name several times as shown. Print it on vellum and cut the vellum into a 2¾" square. Enlarge and print the first initial. Cut it out and use it as a pattern to cut a monogram from cardstock. Tape the monogram to the vellum square. Center the vellum on the card front. Punch two holes, ¾" apart and ¼" from the top of the vellum, through the vellum and card front. Thread the ends of a 4¾" sheer ribbon length through the holes from front to back. Cross the ends, thread them through the holes again from back to front and trim.

For each envelope, use the pattern on page 149 and cut a paper envelope. Fold the side and bottom flaps to the back as indicated by the dashed lines on the pattern and glue them together where they overlap. Glue a ⅝"w paper strip trimmed with the craft scissors along the bottom edge of the envelope flap as shown.

Arrange the tissue in the box. Stack the cards and envelopes, tie sheer ribbon around the stack and place it in the box. Write a message on the tag. Thread the tag onto the center of a length of floss and knot the ends together. Wrapping the ends to the inside, glue two 9" lengths of ⅜"w ribbon to the lid as shown. Tie a bow with another length and glue it to the lid where the ribbons intersect, securing the floss ends of the tag under the bow. Glue the charms to the lid.

PERSONALIZED TAGS WITH GIFT BOX
(shown on page 52)
- 4¾"-tall scalloped tag die and a die-cutting tool
- leather-textured and tan floral scrapbook paper
- brown ink pad
- pinking shears
- floral fabric scrap
- craft glue
- alphabet stencils and stickers
- metal photo corner
- decorative brad and ⅛" dia. silver brads
- assorted charms
- paper twine
- assorted ribbons and fibers
- 2⅜"x4¼" shipping tags
- deckle-edged craft scissors
- grommet and grommet kit
- jewelry tag
- vellum quote
- round-head pin
- sheet of cork
- 4"x4"x5" paper box with lid
- greenery
- small silver ornament
- paper shreds

SCALLOPED TAG
Die-cut a textured paper tag; ink as desired. Zigzag a pinked floral fabric square to the tag. Add an inked stencil monogram and the photo corner. Use a brad to attach charms tied onto paper twine to the tag. Attach a decorative brad through the hole and tightly wrap ribbon around it on the front.

SHIPPING TAGS
Cover one shipping tag with floral scrapbook paper and ink the other. Trim the bottom of the paper-covered tag with the craft scissors. Attach the grommet through the hole in the tag and add the jewelry tag, charms, ribbon and stickers. Tear the long edges of the vellum quote and trim the short edges with the craft scissors. Attach a charm with the pin. Arrange the vellum on a cork piece, spot gluing to secure. Glue the cork to the inked tag. Knot ribbons and fibers through the holes in the tags.

BOX
Tie two 20" ribbon lengths together into a bow around the center of two 8¾" ribbon lengths. Wrapping the ends to the inside, glue the 8¾" lengths to the lid as shown. Tuck the greenery under the bow and glue the ornament to the center of the bow. Place the paper shreds and tags in the box.

BROOCH WITH GIFT BOX
(shown on page 54)
- tracing paper
- illustration board
- silver leaf
- assorted charms
- 15" length of $^1/_8$"w cream ribbon
- craft glue
- assorted beads
- $1^1/_8$" dia., two $^1/_4$" dia. and two $^3/_8$" dia. cream buttons
- watch face
- awl
- wire cutters
- needle-nose pliers
- fine-gauge wire
- cream and textured green cardstock
- 1" pin back
- green acrylic paint
- paintbrush
- $^1/_{16}$" dia. hole punch
- $^3/_8$ yard of $^7/_8$"w green variegated wire-edged ribbon
- 3"x3"x2" white box
- Christmas stamps
- black ink pad
- wood excelsior
- $1^1/_8$ yards of $^3/_{16}$"w green variegated ribbon

1. For the brooch, using the pattern on page 148, cut an oval from illustration board. Follow the manufacturer's instructions to apply silver leaf to the front and sides of the oval.

2. Leaving a streamer on the left back, threading charms onto the ribbon as desired and spot gluing at the back to secure, wrap the cream ribbon around the center of the oval as shown in Fig. 1. Wrap the ribbon to the center back and spot glue, letting the ribbon end dangle for the right streamer. Thread a bead and knot a $^1/_4$" button onto each streamer end; trim the ends.

Fig. 1

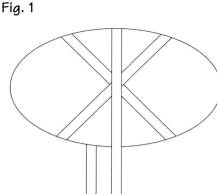

3. Glue the $1^1/_8$" button to the center of the oval and glue the watch face to the button. Use the awl to punch 2 small holes in the oval on each side of the large button. Bending the wire ends at the back of the oval to secure, thread wire through the holes, attaching a $^3/_8$" button and beads to each side.

4. Cut a cream cardstock piece the same size as the oval and glue it to the back. Glue the pin back to the back of the brooch.

5. Cut a $2^7/_8$" textured cardstock square. Refer to *Painting* on page 141 to *Dry Brush* the square with green paint; allow to dry. Punch two holes in the center of the square, $^1/_2$" apart and $^3/_4$" from the top edge. Knotting the ends at the top, wrap the $^7/_8$"w ribbon around the center of the square. Insert the pin through the holes; close the clasp.

6. *Dry Brush* the entire box with green paint; allow to dry. Stamp messages on the outside of the box. Fill the box with excelsior and place the brooch inside. Close the box and tie a 39" length of $^3/_{16}$" ribbon around it.

REINDEER TOWEL AND BATH MITT
(continued from page 63)
BATH MITT
1. Using a photocopier, enlarge the mitt pattern on page 153 to 130% and cut it out. Fold the remaining hand towel in half, matching the short edges. Aligning the bottom edge of the pattern with the short edges of the towel, cut 2 mitts from the folded towel.

2. Using a photocopier, reduce the antler pattern on page 152 to 55%. Using the reduced pattern, cut 2 antlers (one in reverse) from brown felt. For each eye, use the lower case die to cut an "o" from black and white felt. Avoiding the seam allowance and using the outlines from the white die-cuts and the centers from the black die-cuts, Whipstitch (page 140) the antlers and eyes to one mitt as shown.

3. Leaving the bottom edge open, sew the mitt pieces together and turn right side out. Tack the $^3/_4$" pom-pom to the mitt for the nose.

MANICURE GIFT SET
(shown on page 67)
- painter's masking tape
- ivory spray paint for plastic
- manicure set with plastic handles
- green and light green acrylic paints
- paintbrush
- $^1/_4$ yard brown fabric
- pinking shears
- 1 yard of $^5/_8$"w green and white polka-dot grosgrain ribbon
- fabric glue
- vellum tape
- vellum quote
- green scrapbook paper
- decorative-edged craft scissors
- $6^1/_2$"x$3^5/_8$"x$2^5/_8$" white candy box
- brown cardstock
- alphabet stamps
- brown ink pad
- paper shreds

Allow paint to dry after each application.

Working in a well-ventilated area and masking areas that you don't want painted, spray paint the handles of the manicure tools. Remove the tape after the paint has dried. Paint stripes and use the end of the paintbrush handle to add dots on the tool handles with acrylic paints. Cut four $3\frac{1}{4}$"x6" fabric pieces. With the bottom fabric piece wrong side up and the remaining pieces right side up, stack and sew the fabric pieces together $3/8$" from the edges; pink the edges. Arrange the tools across the fabric. Center a $6\frac{3}{4}$" ribbon length across the tools and pin the ribbon to the fabric between the tools. Remove the tools and sew down the ribbon at the pins. Remove the pins and glue the ribbon ends to the back.

Tape the vellum quote to the paper, cut it out with craft scissors and glue it to the inside of the box lid. Cut a small paper oval and a large cardstock oval. Glue the ovals together and stamp a message on the center.

Fill the box with paper shreds and place the manicure set inside. Close the lid and wrap a 28" ribbon length around the box, tying a bow at the top. Glue the ovals to the front of the box over the ribbon.

PENNY SACK AND GIFT BOX
(shown on page 68)
- star background and holiday message stamps
- brown ink pad
- penny sack
- 3"x3"x2" brown gift box
- deckle-edged craft scissors
- red, tan, green, red-checked and off-white cardstock
- green chalk
- craft glue
- tracing paper
- red seed beads
- $1/8$" dia. hole punch
- red jute

Stamp stars all over the sack and box. Use craft scissors to cut cardstock squares as follows: $2\frac{1}{2}$" red, $2\frac{1}{4}$" tan, 2" green, $1\frac{3}{4}$" red-checked and $1\frac{1}{2}$" off-white. Chalk the edges of the off-white square. Layer and glue the squares on the bag front. Cut an off-white cardstock tag for the box. Using the pattern on page 157, cut 2 green holly leaves each for the box and bag. Chalk the tag edges. Glue the tag to red cardstock and cut the cardstock slightly larger than the tag. Stamp a message and glue holly leaves and seed bead "berries" on the tag and bag. Punch two holes, $3/4$" apart, through the top of the bag front and back. Thread jute through the holes and tie into a bow at the front. Punch a hole at the top of the tag, thread jute through the hole and knot the ends together. Tie jute around the box and tuck the tag under the jute.

EARRINGS WITH GIFT TAG
(shown on page 69)
Dress up an ordinary shipping tag with scrapbook paper, ribbon and red zigzag stitches for a classy gift tag for handmade earrings. Stamp Santa on cream cardstock and color with colored pencils. Tear the cardstock and sew it to a torn red cardstock piece. Glue Santa to the tag along with crocheted leaves and red buttons. Cut an arrow-shaped scrapbook paper tag and add red stitches, a stamped message, red seed bead "berries" and leaves colored with a pencil. Stamp the date on the gift tag and attach the paper tag and a knotted ribbon length with a brad. Knot ribbon and fiber through the hole in the gift tag.

For each earring, thread assorted beads onto a $1\frac{1}{2}$" eye pin. Use round-nose pliers to make a tight loop at the end of the pin near the bottom bead. Trim the excess wire with wire cutters. Attach the eye pin to a shank earwire. Punch tiny holes in the tag and attach the earrings to the tag through the holes.

GENERAL INSTRUCTIONS

EMBROIDERY STITCHES

BLANKET STITCH: Referring to Fig. 1, bring the needle up at 1. Keeping the thread below the point of the needle, go down at 2 and come up at 3. Continue working as shown in Fig. 2.

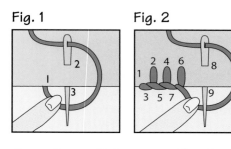

Fig. 1 **Fig. 2**

CHAIN STITCH: Referring to Fig. 3, bring the needle up at 1; take the needle down at 1 to form a loop. Bring the needle up at 2; take the needle down at 2 to form a second loop. Bring the needle up at 3 and repeat as in Fig. 4. Anchor the last chain with a small straight stitch.

Fig. 3 **Fig. 4**

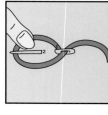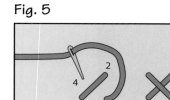

CROSS STITCH: Bring the needle up at 1 and go down at 2. Come up at 3 and go down at 4 (Fig. 5).

Fig. 5

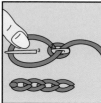

FRENCH KNOT: Referring to Fig. 6, bring the needle up at 1. Wrap the floss once around the needle and insert the needle at 2, holding the floss end with non-stitching fingers. Tighten the knot; then, pull the needle through the fabric, holding the floss until it must be released. For a larger knot, use more strands; wrap only once.

Fig. 6

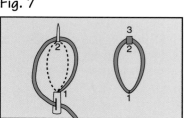

LAZY DAISY STITCH: Bring the needle up at 1; take the needle down at 1 to form a loop and bring the needle up at 2. Keeping the loop below the point of the needle (Fig. 7), take the needle down at 3 to anchor the loop.

Fig. 7

RUNNING STITCH: Referring to Fig. 8, make a series of straight stitches with the stitch length equal to the space between stitches.

Fig. 8

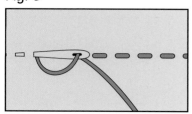

STRAIGHT STITCH: Referring to Fig. 9, come up at 1 and go down at 2.

Fig. 9

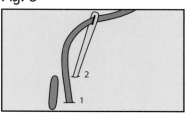

WHIPSTITCH: Bring the needle up at 1; take the thread around the edge of the fabric and bring the needle up at 2. Continue stitching along the edge of the fabric (Fig. 10).

Fig. 10

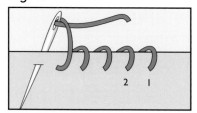

MAKING PATTERNS

When the entire pattern is shown, place tracing paper over the pattern and draw over the lines. For a more durable pattern, use a permanent marker to draw over the pattern on stencil plastic.

When only half the pattern is shown (indicated by a solid blue line on the pattern), fold the tracing paper in half. Place the fold along the solid blue line and trace the pattern half. Turn the folded paper over and draw over the traced lines on the remaining side. Unfold the pattern and cut it out.

PAINTING

DRY BRUSHING: Do not dip the brush in water. Dip a stipple brush or old paintbrush in paint; wipe most of the paint off onto a dry paper towel. Lightly rub the brush across the surface. Repeat as needed.

KNIT

ABBREVIATIONS

cm	centimeters
K	knit
mm	millimeters
P	purl
PSSO	pass slipped stitch over
st(s)	stitch(es)
tog	together

★ — work instructions following ★ as many **more** times as indicated in addition to the first time.

( ) or [ ] — work enclosed instructions **as many** times as specified by the number immediately following **or** work all enclosed instructions in the stitch or space indicated **or** contains explanatory remarks.

colon (:) — the number(s) given after a colon at the end of a row or round denote(s) the number of stitches you should have on that row or round.

GAUGE

Exact gauge is essential for proper fit. Before beginning your project, make the sample swatch given in the individual instructions in the yarn and needle specified. After completing the swatch, measure it, counting your stitches and rows or rounds carefully. If your swatch is larger or smaller than specified, make another, changing needle size to get the correct gauge. Keep trying until you find the size needles that will give you the specified gauge.

KNIT 2 TOGETHER

(abbreviated K2 tog)
Insert the right needle into the **front** of the first two stitches on the left needle as if to **knit** (Fig. 1); then, **knit** them together as if they were one stitch.

Fig. 1

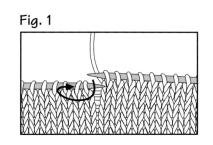

PURL 2 TOGETHER

(abbreviated P2 tog)
Insert the right needle into the **front** of the first two stitches on the left needle as if to **purl** (Fig. 2); then, **purl** them together as if they were one stitch.

Fig. 2

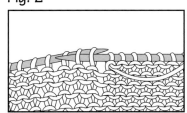

SLIP 1, KNIT 1, PASS SLIPPED STITCH OVER

(abbreviated slip 1, K1, PSSO)
Slip one stitch as if to **knit** (Fig. 3a). Knit the next stitch. With the left needle, bring the slipped stitch over the knit stitch (Fig. 3b) and off the needle.

Fig. 3a   **Fig. 3b**

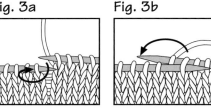

PICKING UP STITCHES

When instructed to pick up stitches, insert the needle from the **front** to the **back** under two strands at the edge of the worked piece (Fig. 4). Put the yarn around the needle as if to **knit**; then, bring the needle with the yarn back through the stitch to the right side, resulting in a stitch on the needle. Repeat this along the edge, picking up the required number of stitches. A crochet hook may be helpful to pull the yarn through.

Fig. 4

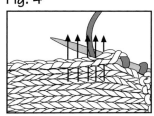

WEAVING SEAMS

With the **right** side of both pieces facing you and the edges even, sew through both sides once to secure the seam. Insert the needle under the bar **between** the first and second stitches on the row and pull the yarn through (Fig. 5). Insert the needle under the next bar on the second side. Repeat from side to side, being careful to match rows. If the edges are different lengths, it may be necessary to insert the needle under two bars at one edge.

Fig. 5

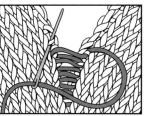

CROCHET

ABBREVIATIONS
ch(s)   chain(s)
cm   centimeters
dc   double crochet(s)
mm   millimeters
sp(s)   space(s)

( ) — work all enclosed instructions in the stitch or space indicated **or** contains explanatory remarks.

GAUGE
Exact gauge is essential for proper fit. Before beginning your project, make the sample swatch given in the individual instructions in the yarn and hook specified. After completing the swatch, measure it, counting stitches and rows or rounds carefully. If your swatch is larger or smaller than specified, make another, changing hook size to get the correct gauge. Keep trying until you find the size hook that will give you the specified gauge.

MAKING A FABRIC CIRCLE
Matching right sides, fold the fabric square in half from top to bottom and again from left to right. Tie one end of a length of string to a fabric marking pen; insert a thumbtack through the string at the length indicated in the project instructions. Insert the thumbtack through the folded corner of the fabric. Holding the tack in place and keeping the string taut, mark the cutting line (Fig. 1).

Fig. 1

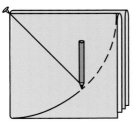

CONTINUOUS BIAS BINDING
1. Fold the fabric square in half diagonally; cut on the fold to make 2 triangles.

2. With the right sides together and using a ¼" seam allowance, sew the triangles together (Fig. 1). Press the seam allowances open.

Fig. 1

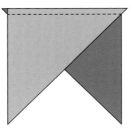

3. On the wrong side of the fabric, draw lines the width given in the project instructions, parallel to the long edges (Fig. 2). Cut off any remaining fabric less than this width.

Fig. 2

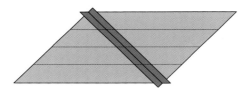

4. With the right sides inside, bring the short edges together to form a tube; match the raw edges so the first drawn line of the top section meets the second drawn line of the bottom section (Fig. 3).

Fig. 3

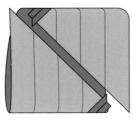

5. Carefully pin the edges together by inserting pins through the drawn lines at the point where the drawn lines intersect, making sure the pins go through the intersections on both sides. Using a ¼" seam allowance, sew the edges together; press the seam allowances open.

6. To cut a continuous strip, begin cutting along the first drawn line (Fig. 4). Continue cutting along the drawn line around the tube.

Fig. 4

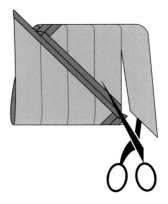

7. Trim each end of the bias strip as shown in Fig. 5.

Fig. 5

MERRY TAG
(page 19)

I BELIEVE TAG
(page 16)

Believe

MERRY TAG
(page 19)

S'MORE BARS
PACKAGE
(page 72)

CHRISTMAS TAG
(page 19)

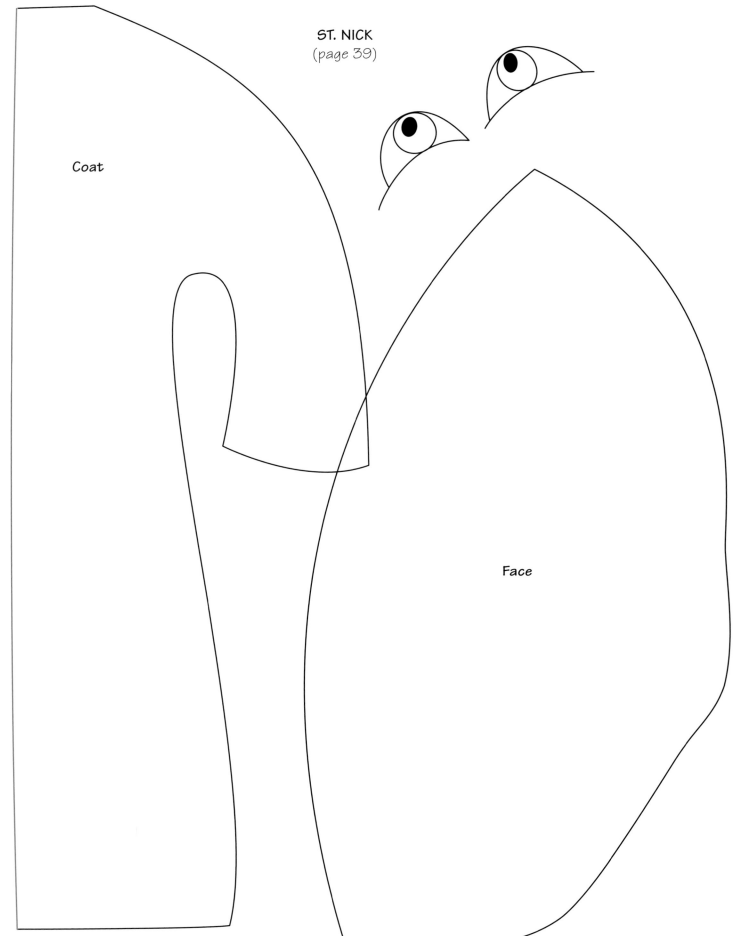

ST. NICK
(page 39)

Coat

Face

144

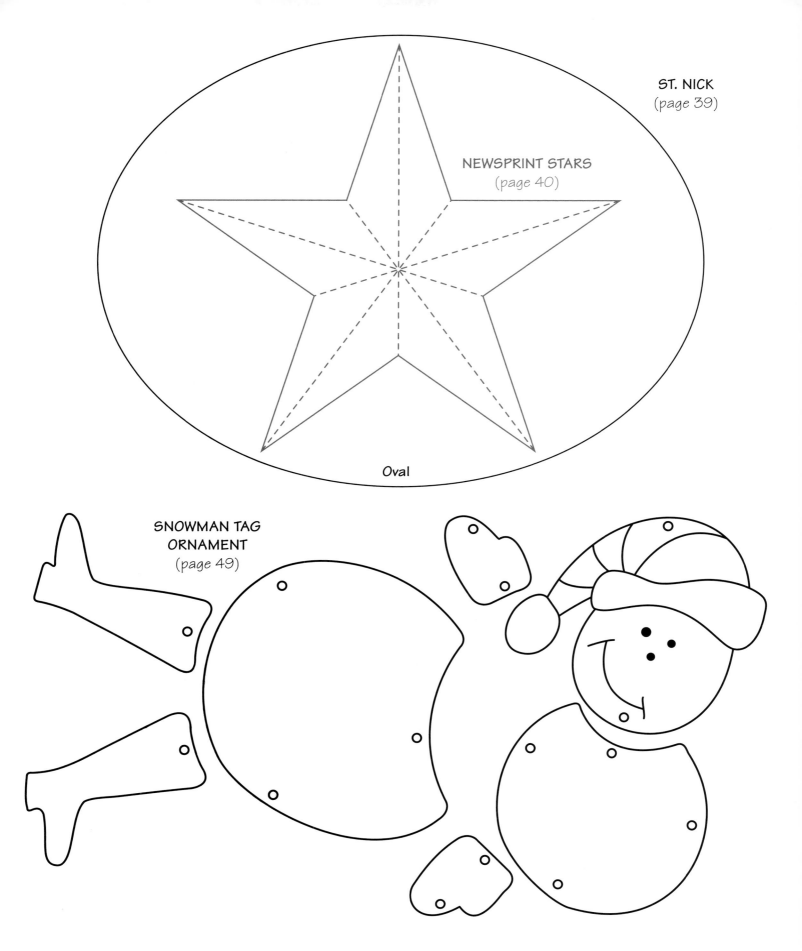

ST. NICK
(page 39)

NEWSPRINT STARS
(page 40)

Oval

SNOWMAN TAG
ORNAMENT
(page 49)

BIRCH-FRAMED CABIN ART
(page 42)

SANTA DOORMAT
(page 65)

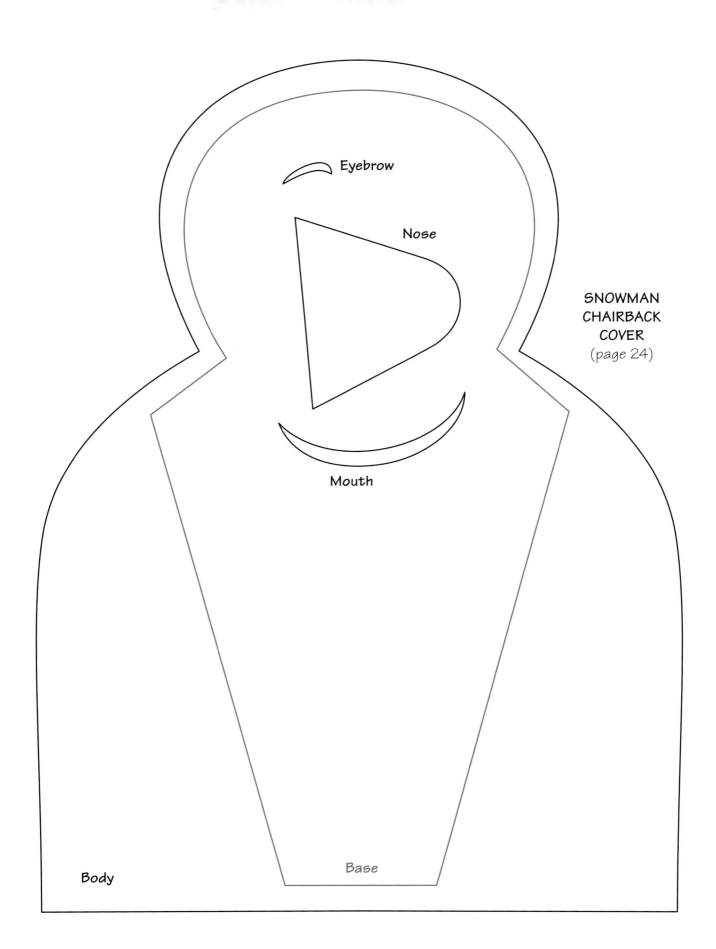

Eyebrow

Nose

SNOWMAN
CHAIRBACK
COVER
(page 24)

Mouth

Body

Base

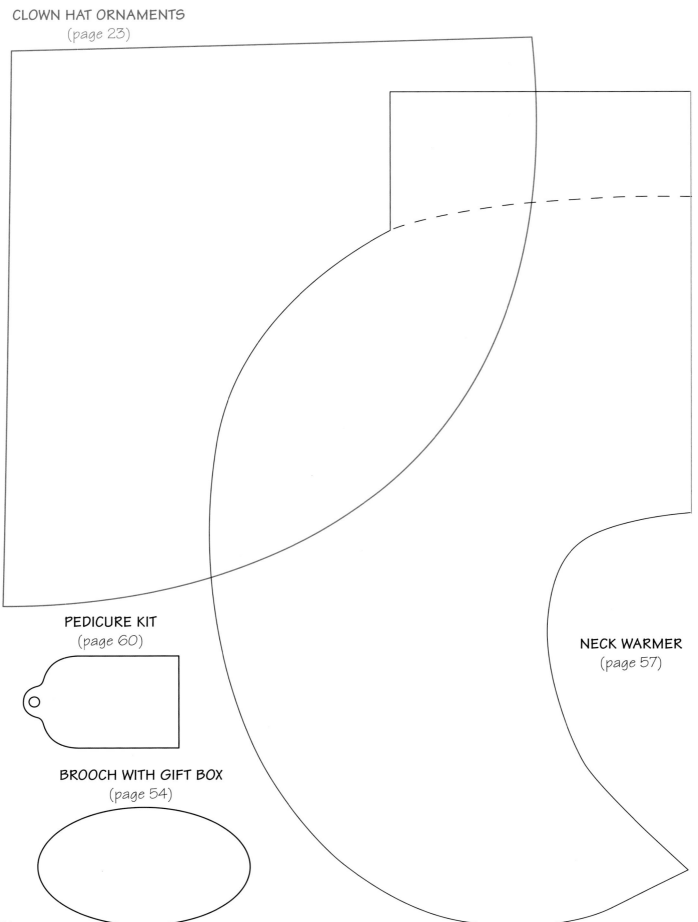

CLOWN HAT ORNAMENTS
(page 23)

PEDICURE KIT
(page 60)

NECK WARMER
(page 57)

BROOCH WITH GIFT BOX
(page 54)

BOXED PERSONALIZED CARD SET
(page 53)

—— Chain Stitch

⟋ Lazy Daisies

● French Knots

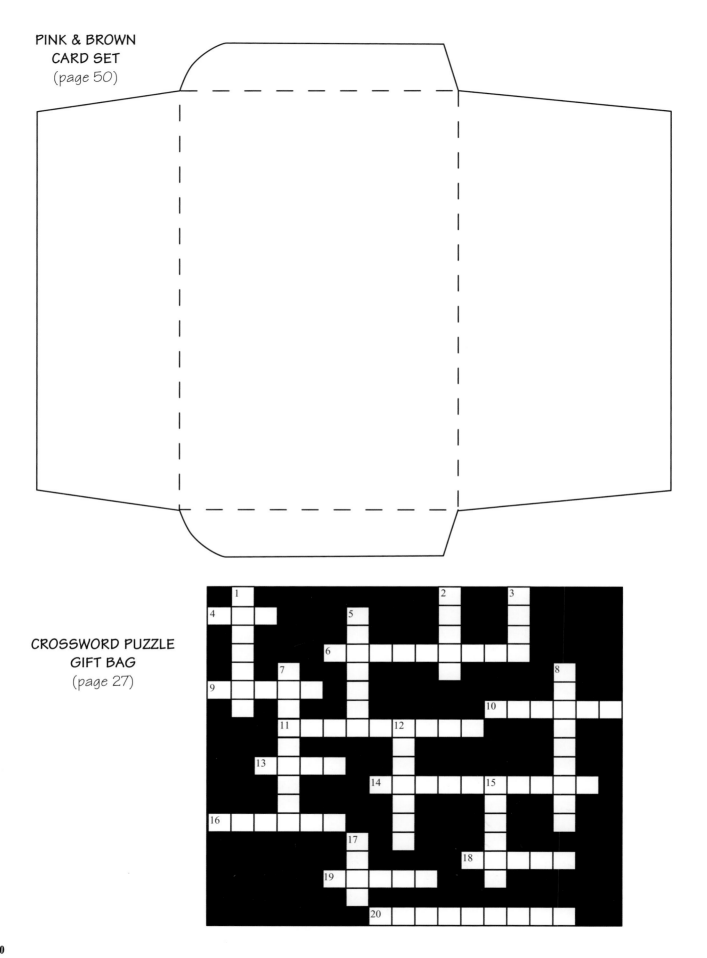

PINK & BROWN
CARD SET
(page 50)

CROSSWORD PUZZLE
GIFT BAG
(page 27)

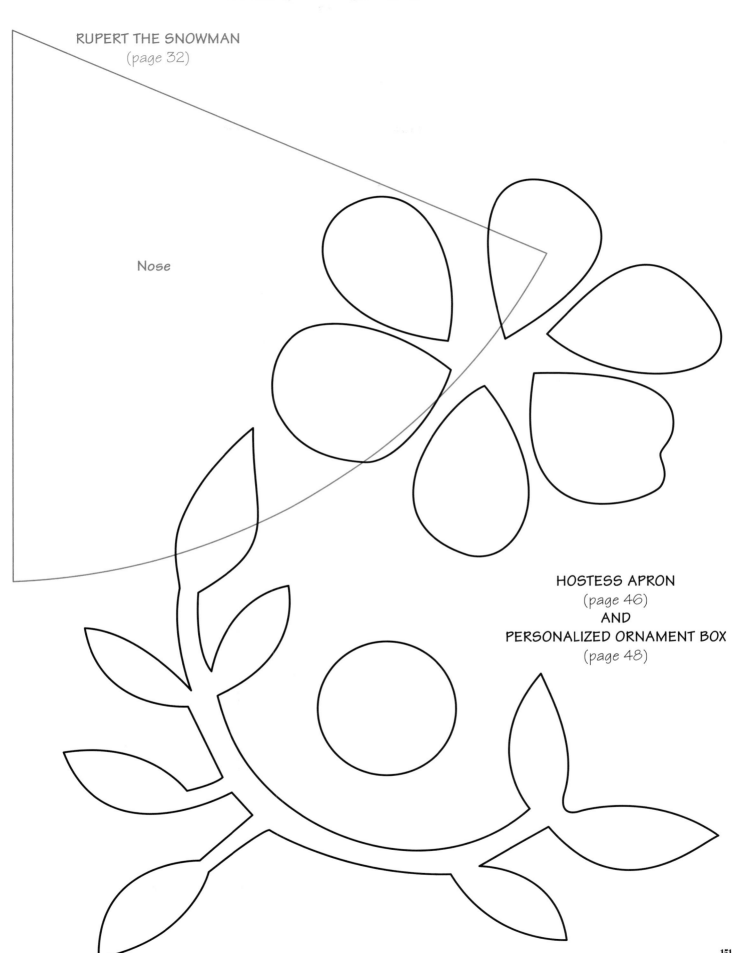

RUPERT THE SNOWMAN
(page 32)

Nose

HOSTESS APRON
(page 46)
AND
PERSONALIZED ORNAMENT BOX
(page 48)

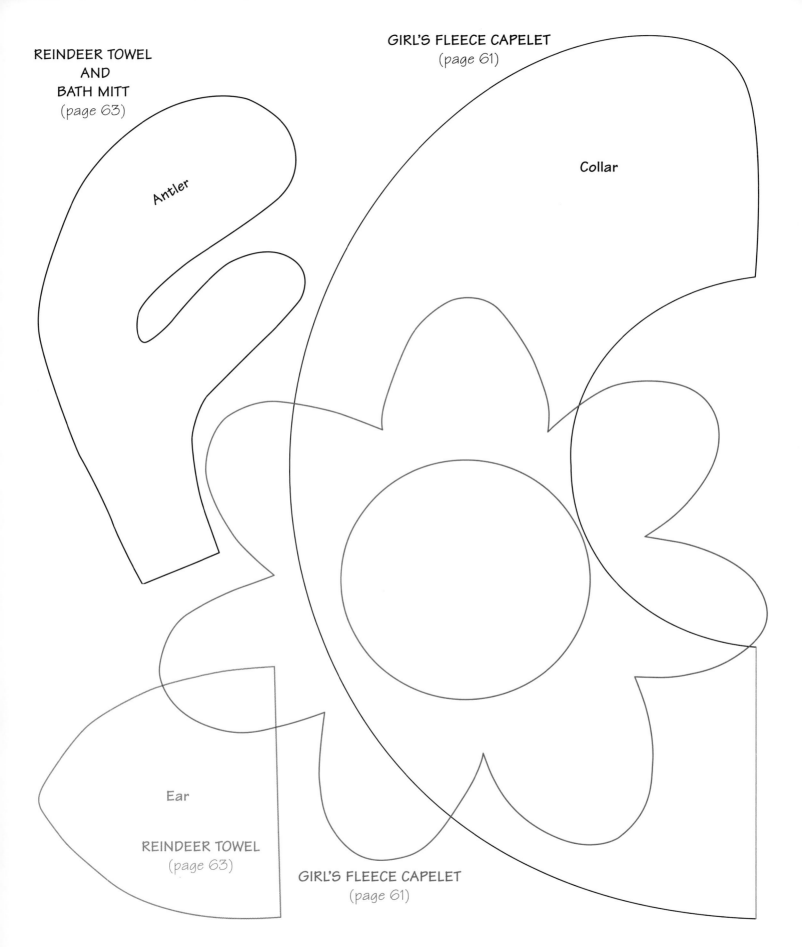

REINDEER TOWEL
AND
BATH MITT
(page 63)

Antler

GIRL'S FLEECE CAPELET
(page 61)

Collar

Ear

REINDEER TOWEL
(page 63)

GIRL'S FLEECE CAPELET
(page 61)

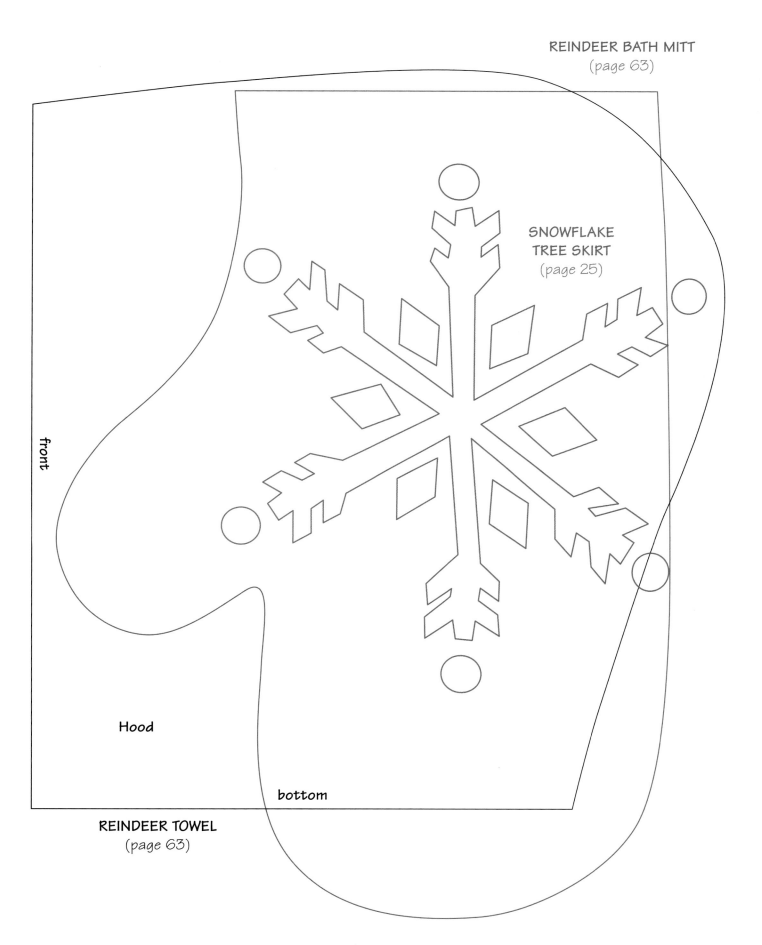

SNOWFLAKE
TREE SKIRT
(page 25)

front

Hood

bottom

REINDEER TOWEL
(page 63)

DOG ALBUM
(page 64)

CAT ALBUM
(page 64)

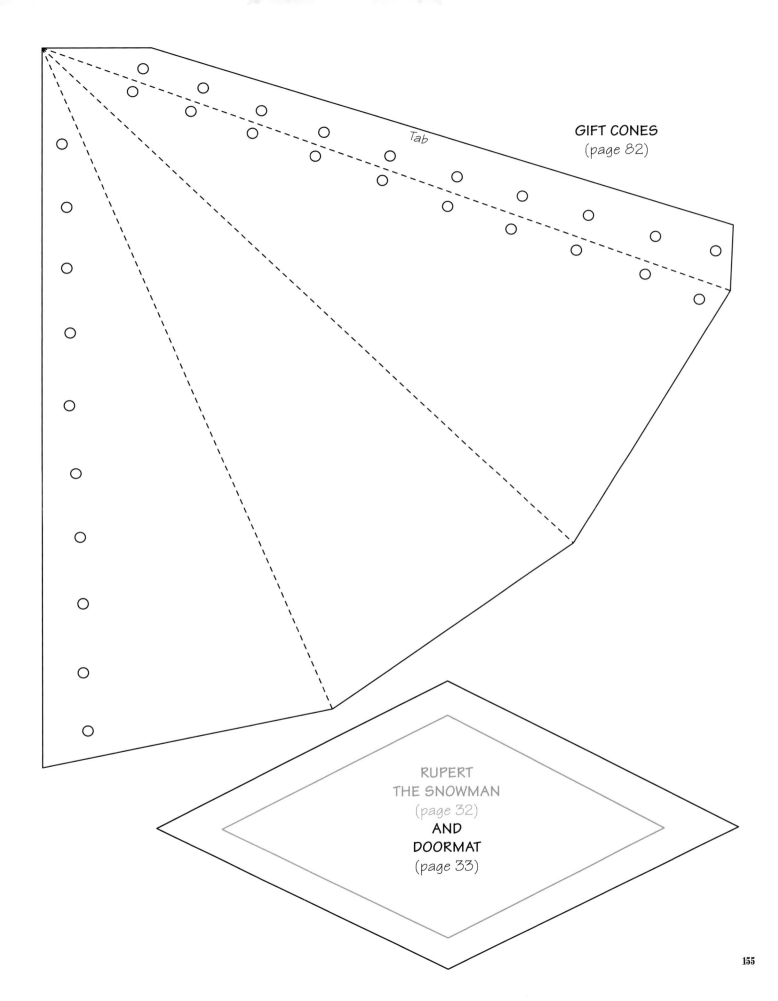

GIFT CONES
(page 82)

Tab

RUPERT
THE SNOWMAN
(page 32)
AND
DOORMAT
(page 33)

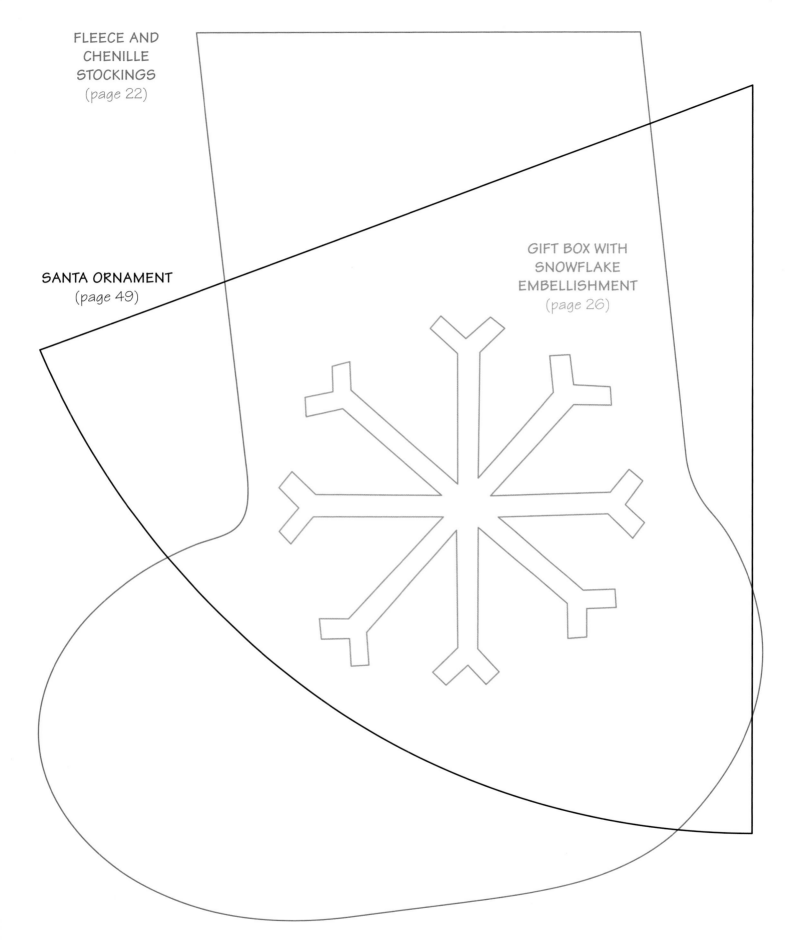

FLEECE AND
CHENILLE
STOCKINGS
(page 22)

SANTA ORNAMENT
(page 49)

GIFT BOX WITH
SNOWFLAKE
EMBELLISHMENT
(page 26)

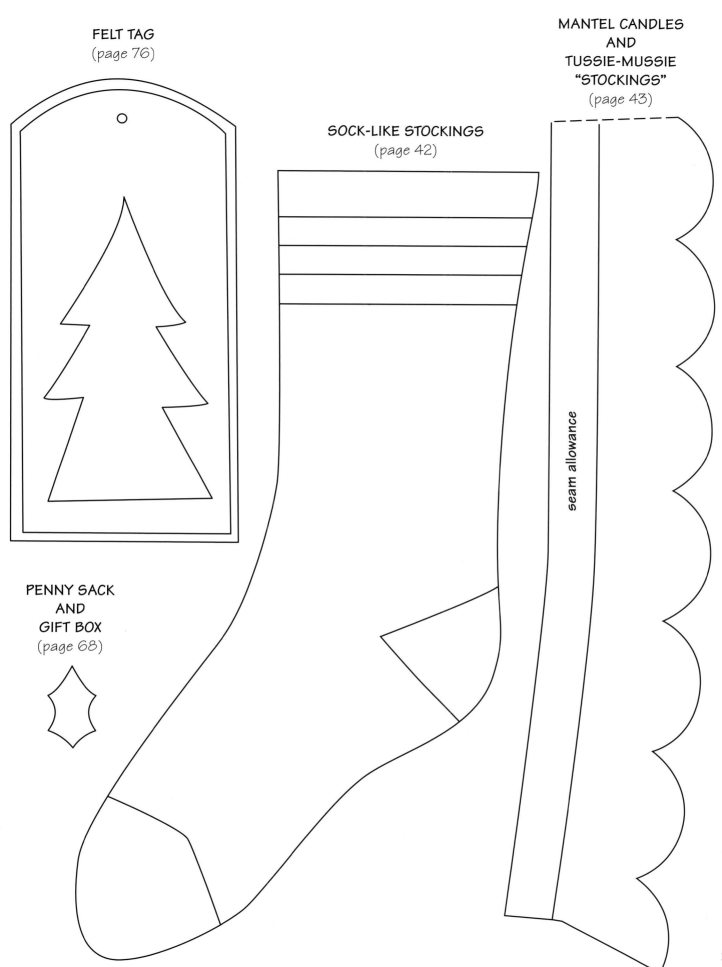

FELT TAG
(page 76)

MANTEL CANDLES
AND
TUSSIE-MUSSIE
"STOCKINGS"
(page 43)

SOCK-LIKE STOCKINGS
(page 42)

PENNY SACK
AND
GIFT BOX
(page 68)

seam allowance

PROJECT INDEX

RECIPE INDEX

Credits

We want to extend a warm thank you to the people who allowed us to photograph some of our projects at their homes: Nancy Appleton, Alda Ellis, Cheryl Johnson, August & Christy Myers, Liz Rice and Leighton Weeks.

We want to especially thank photographers Jerry R. Davis of Jerry Davis Photography, Mark Mathews Photography, Ken West Photography and Larry Pennington Studios, all of Little Rock, Arkansas, for their excellent work.

We would like to recognize the following companies for providing some of the materials and tools we used to make our projects: David Textiles for fleece; Die Cuts with a View for Monogram Stacks; DonJer Products for Soft Flock fibers and adhesive; Meltie Felties for wool felt; Sizzix for die-cutters and dies; and Delta Technical Coatings for some of the paints used.

If these cozy Christmas ideas have inspired you to look for more Gooseberry Patch® publications, treat yourself to a Gooseberry Patch product catalog, which is filled with cookbooks, candles, enamelware, bowls, gourmet goodies and hundreds of other country collectibles. For a subscription to "A Country Store in Your Mailbox®," visit www.gooseberrypatch.com.

Next to acquiring good friends, the best acquisition is that of good books.

– CALEB COLTON –